Understanding Financial Services from a Customer Perspective

Claire Bateson

Financial World Publishing
4–9 Burgate Lane
Canterbury
Kent
CT1 2XJ

T 01227 818687
F 01227 479641
E editorial@ifslearning.com

Financial World Publishing publications are published by The Chartered Institute of Bankers, a non-profit making registered educational charity.

Typeset by the Alden Group, Oxford.
Printed by Antony Rowe Ltd., Chippenham

ISBN 0-85297-636-4

Contents

Contents

Unit 1

The role of financial services institutions in the wider business environment

The aim of this module is to enable you to:

- *Explain the main theories of macro-economics:*
  - ○ *The money supply.*
  - ○ *Inflation.*
  - ○ *Interest rates.*
  - ○ *The implications for customers and their finances.*
  - ○ *The effect of the European Monetary policy on the UK financial services providers.*
- *Identify the major financial services organisations and the roles they play*
- *Explain the concept of social responsibility*

Introduction to macro-economics

Macro-economics is concerned with looking at the bigger picture of all decisions made by individuals, business and government. The word 'macro' comes from the Greek, meaning large. Macro-economics examines the national and international effect of all these collective decisions and ways in which the state manages its economy. Figure 1.1 shows the different branches of economics.

It is important to appreciate how this environment works, as it can affect individuals, the organisations they work for and the governments they vote for. It can affect you, through the profit your employer makes and the amount of salary they can afford to pay. It can also affect you through the amount of tax you pay to support

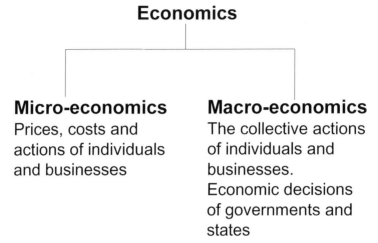

Figure 1.1 *Different branches of economics.*

government policies. In the same way your customers will be affected and understanding the pressures they are under is a key part of your role.

Let us look next at the key macro-environmental influences:

- *Political/legal – these can be in such areas as:*
  - Monopolies legislation *– this can prevent large organisations from merging and taking advantage of holding too large a customer base and, therefore, having too much power. The Competition Commission has been active in the financial services arena in the past few years monitoring proposed mergers, i.e. between Royal Bank of Scotland and NatWest.*
  - Taxation policy *– at every budget in March, new taxation rates are announced. This can be through direct tax such as income tax, or indirect tax such as value-added tax (VAT) or tobacco tax on cigarettes.*
  - Government stability *– constantly changing governments lead to raised uncertainty at home and abroad over the stability of the country's economy.*
  - Employment law *– new legislation can affect organisations and their employees. The Minimum wage rulings effectively raised the costs of production across industry. In the same way stakeholder pensions will affect employers' obligations to their staff.*
- *Sociocultural factors – for example:*
  - Population demographics *– although in Britain there is a decreasing population, the demand for housing is increasing. This is because the number of households are increasing through divorce and the increase of single or lone parents.*

- ○ **Lifestyle changes** – *more people work outside of the traditional office hours and, therefore, need to be able to access goods and services at times to suit them. This has led to Sunday opening, 24-hour shopping and the growth of the Internet for purchasing goods and services.*

- ○ **Levels of education** – *education is open to everyone in Britain and attendance at university or college is no longer the privilege of the upper classes. Better education has meant that people have more choice over their careers.*

- • *Technological – these can be in such areas as:*
  - ○ **New developments and discoveries** – *there is competitive advantage in something that is 'new'. This is, therefore, a drive by industry to make new inventions and innovations and be ahead of the game.*
  - ○ **Rates of obsolescence** – *because of the drive for new inventions, technology evolves at a very high rate. A new mobile phone model that is capable of far more, will have superseded a phone you bought 12 months ago.*

- • *Economic factors – for example:*
  - ○ **Unemployment** – *this has been a factor that successive governments have been measured on and is seen as key indicator of prosperity. For the individual trying to find a job when there is high unemployment and everyone else is looking for work, it is very hard.*
  - ○ **Disposable income** – *the more money people have in their pockets the more they are able to spend on their leisure and the more confident they feel. Overall this can have positive effect on the economy and the businesses within it. However, this can lead to inflation (see section 2.0) and the government can take steps to reduce inflation by increasing taxes so reducing the amount of disposable income people have.*
  - ○ **Interest rates, money supply and inflation** – *areas, which will be looked at in more detail in the next section.*

Think

There are four types of factors which affect the macro-environment:

Political/legal
Sociocultural
Technological
Economic

Think about the following questions:

What macro-environmental factors affect your organisation?

Which are the most important factors at the moment?

Which factors are likely to become important in the next few years?

All these areas are uncertain, and they can be said to be dynamic and complex. The business environment is no longer simple and stable, as it has been perceived to be in the past. The success of an organisation depends on how well it copes with these levels of uncertainty. Success also depends on how well trends in the macro-environment are predicted and acted upon.

The next sections are about some of the key components of how the government and the Bank of England manages the economy and the tools it uses to do so.

1.0
The money supply

1.1   We have seen that the government will try to control the economy by increasing taxes and regulating the amount of government spending. This is called *Fiscal Policy*. The other way that government regulates the economy is by *Monetary Policy*. This means controlling the *price* and *supply* of money.

The price of money relates to interest rates, which we will look at later. The supply of money is about the amount of money in circulation. Before going into this in detail let us first consider what we actually mean by money.

'Money' means more than just cash.

Note

Make a note of all the different ways that you use to pay for goods and services.

You have probably come up with quite a long list. Not only do we use notes and coins, but also various cards, debit cards like Switch, credit cards like Visa or MasterCard, and cheques for bank and building society accounts.

Money can be defined as a medium of exchange by which we trade goods and services. It can also be a way of accumulating wealth so that we can save up to buy goods and services in the future. Another way of purchasing what we want is to buy now and pay later – credit. Credit is a vital component of the modern monetary and financial system. In order to be useful for day-to-day living these various forms of money must provide a consistent measure of comparative value and be acceptable to everyone.

1.2   What constitutes money centres around the concept of *liquidity*. This is the degree to which whatever *assets* you hold can be converted into money without penalty. The liquidity spectrum if drawn would look something like Figure 1.2.

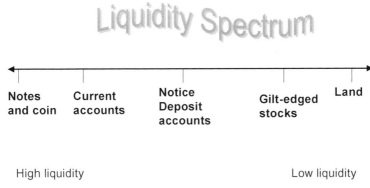

Figure 1.2 *Liquidity spectrum.*

At what point on the spectrum could we say that an asset is not liquid enough to be called money? There is no definite answer to this, so in practice the chosen point may depend on the purpose for which the definition of money is to be used.

1.3   To clarify this for macro-economic and measurement purposes the government uses the following guidelines:

- **M0** *comprises of only notes and coin plus the banks' operational deposits (those which are used for* clearing *activities between the banks) held with the Bank of England.*
- **M2** *includes M0 plus customers' current and deposit accounts that require no or little notice of withdrawal. It is a measure of funds for day-to-day use and M0 and M2 are known as* narrow money.

- **M4** *is an even wider definition with includes M2 and money held for investment purposes. This is known as* broad money.

1.4   Having defined what we mean by money now let us look at two important principles related to the money supply and the money cycle. These are the *volume* of money and the *velocity* of money. To help explain this the diagram in Figure 1.3 shows the money cycle with injections and leakages of money.

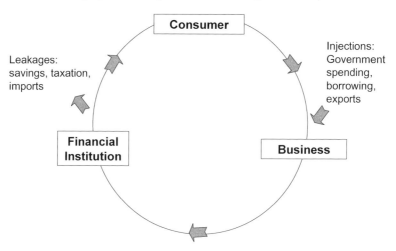

Figure 1.3 *Money cycle. Note leakages and injections can occur at any points on the cycle.*

In simple terms, if you go to the supermarket to buy your groceries and pay by cash, your money is paid into the supermarket's bank account. The cash is then available for withdrawal by someone else. If the money supply (M0) is reduced, by the destruction soiled notes, the financial institution may become short of notes and have to contact the supermarket to ask them to pay their cash in earlier than they would normally. You can see that in this instance the velocity or speed at which cash moves round the cycle increases because the volume or amount of money has decreased.

However, this theory only holds true to a point, as in reality the system is not closed and there are leakages and injections of cash, which the diagram in Figure 1.3 shows. This is why the government and the Bank of England regard notes and coins as a very small component of the overall monetary system. Customers borrowing from the financial institutions can have a powerful influence on the economy as a whole and the regulators may wish to control the amount of credit being created.

When times are difficult the financial institutions can contribute to recovery by encouraging businesses to go ahead with new products (through lending) that create jobs. During a period of *boom*, when the economy is working to full capacity, lending to businesses could exaggerate demand and lead to inflation. This would happen if the economy was to *overheat* and demand for goods and services exceeded supply, which in turn could lead to higher prices.

1.5   The government monitors the level of economic activity in order to keep an acceptable balance between the level of employment and the rate of inflation (which we will look at in the next section). At the same time the government is aiming to achieve reasonable *balance of payments* equilibrium between imports and exports and to maintain a reasonable rate of economic growth, which is good for businesses and individuals alike. This means that society in general can enjoy an increased standard of living.

2.0
Inflation

2.1   We have seen that the creation of credit (financial institution lending/ customer borrowing) helps to increase the money supply and make the economy work. It increases people's ability to spend. If the ability to spend is not controlled, however, this can lead to inflation. One group of prominent economic theorists, known as *Monetarists*, believe that control of the growth of money supply is the most important economic function of government.

So, what is inflation? It can be defined simply as 'a rise in the general price of goods and services'. It is a year-on-year overall rise in prices or, from another viewpoint, the year-on-year reduction in the value of money. A £1 coin will be worth less this year compared to last year, in terms of spending power, by an amount equal to the rate of inflation.

Think

Consider the following:

> Think back to ten years ago. How much did something you bought regularly cost, (newspaper, sweets or a bottle of milk) compared with how much it costs today?

2.2   There are two main causes of inflation:

- Cost-push inflation *where the costs to industry are increased and these costs are passed onto the consumer. In terms of financial services organisations this is where* the costs of lending are increased by raising interest rates or increases in other costs such as wages or premises costs.

- Demand-led inflation where there is an excess of spending power in the economy. This is not only from increased customer borrowing but also from tax cuts, high wage increases and falling unemployment. It can be described as too much money chasing too few goods.

2.3   There are a number of ways in which inflation is measured:

- Retail Price Index (RPI), which is the most commonly quoted measure of inflation in the UK. It is based on a combination of the prices of a basket of goods and services designed to be representative of the outgoings of an average family. The RPI is a measure of the headline rate of inflation and includes mortgage interest.
- Underlying rate of inflation uses the same basis as RPI except that it excludes the effect of mortgage interest.
- Wholesale Prices Index is based on the prices of raw material and wholesale prices charged by manufacturers.
- National Average Earning Index reflects changes in the levels of earned income in the UK. It generally rises more quickly than the RPI indicating an increase in the standard of living.

Note

Make a note of your answers.

For the following changes in the economic environment, say whether each of the changes is most likely to be inflationary or deflationary:

- A cut in the basic rate of income tax

- An increase in interest rates

- An increase in unemployment

- A cut in government spending

- The government no longer controls inflation and interest rates directly. It now sets the Bank of England inflation targets based on the above measures and the Bank takes steps to control inflation on the government's behalf. It is also tasked with *supporting the government's economic policy including objectives for growth and employment. Interest rates are set by the Bank of England's Monetary Policy Committee (MPC) and the MPC has to judge what interest rate is necessary to meet a target for overall inflation in the economy. The Bank implements these decisions through its financial markets operations.*

2.4   Having seen how inflation can be controlled we should now consider the implications for customers.

Note

Make a note of your answers

1   *What is the effect of low inflation on a family of four?*

2   *What is the effect of high inflation on a pensioner living from their savings?*

3   *What are the implications for a business that is borrowing a large sum of money in a period of high inflation when typically interest rates are also high?*

4   *During periods of low inflation how successful are requests for high wage rises likely to be received by an employer?*

There are some problems that the effects of inflation can cause for individuals and businesses:

- *Inflation erodes the value of savings because the purchasing power of capital is reduced. So, therefore, the pensioner in question 2 above will be disadvantaged by a period of high inflation.*
- *Trade debtors (those who owe money although they are not required to pay interest on it as it is part of a purchasing agreement) can gain at the expense of the*

creditors (those to whom the money is owed). This is because the relative value of cash is reducing compared to the value of the goods they have purchased.

- *As in question 3 above, periods of high inflation are often accompanied by periods of high interest rates resulting in increased costs of borrowing. This will mean that the business will have increased costs of production and will need to recover these costs somehow.*

- *Inflation affects the distribution of income. Those with a strong wage earning capability gain over those on relatively fixed incomes, such as pensioners or students. During periods of low inflation, as in question 4, organisations are likely to be resistant to claims for high wage rises because there will be little justification to meet increased costs of living.*

- *A country's balance of payments (level of imports and exports) position can be affected during times of high inflation, as the goods and services it exports become dearer in comparison with its imports. Over time it will make that country's businesses less price competitive in international business transactions.*

- *Variability or erratically increasing prices add to the uncertainty of the economic environment. This can have a negative affect on business and consumer confidence and could delay investment and spending.*

2.5   It has been mentioned at the beginning of the section that controlling inflation is one of the key actions in influencing the economy. For the last 25 years or more it has been a major priority of British and other governments to minimise the levels of inflation. A typical target is to keep inflation at between 1% and 4% per annum. This aim has not always been achieved. In the early 1990s the rate of inflation in the UK was around 10% and during the 1970s it rose to as high as almost 30% at one point. Some other countries have fared much worse with inflation rates of 1000% or more having been experienced during economic crises. This is known as *hyper-inflation.*

3.0
Interest rates

3.1   Interest rates can be defined quite simply as the *price of money.* In particular, it reflects the cost of borrowing money and the reward for lending it.

- *To savers it is the reward given by financial institutions for the use of savers' money. They receive* credit interest.
- *To borrowers, it is the price they must pay the lender for the use of funds for a certain period of time. They are deducted* debit interest.

Think

Consider the following:

> Why is it that the amount of interest paid to borrowers is less than the amount of interest charged to borrowers?

3.2   It was mentioned in 1.1 that a way of purchasing what we want is to buy now and pay later is credit. How does this come into being? How is credit created? The remainder of this section looks at how credit is created and the effect of interest rates.

3.3   Financial services institutions aim to make profit for their shareholders and one way of doing this is by lending out some of the funds they are holding on behalf of their savers. These institutions lend to individuals, companies, public bodies, the money markets and the government. With a wise lending policy a financial services institution can increase its profits by increasing its lending. So, how much can a financial services organisation lend and how much credit can it create? The answers to these two questions appear to be the same, but they are not as you will see later.

3.4   Most financial services organisations needs to keep a certain portion of their funds liquid (in notes and/or coin) to meet daily requirements such as cash withdrawals. However, most current account customers use cheques, direct debits and plastic cards for many of their transactions. So the institutions find that the amount of liquid funds they need is quite small in relation to the total amount of deposits they hold. The remainder can then be lent to other customers and the interest that they will pay contributes to the institutions profits. The differential between the interest rates charged is the income gained by this method.

Think

Think about this problem

> At the turn of the 21st century many people were worried about the effects of the Millennium bug on computer systems. Some people felt that they should withdraw all their cash from their accounts just in case something went wrong. What would have been the implications for ATMs and branches if all their customers had done this?

3.5   Here is an example to show why the answers to the two questions in 3.3 are not the same. The percentage of funds deposited, which a financial services institution considers sufficient to cover customers' cash withdrawals is known as the *reserve asset ratio*. For the purposes of this example we will assume that a ratio of 10% is being used. Consider this theoretical chain of events which is set in motion by Mr Black depositing a cheque for £10,000 into his building society account:

- *The building society can lend the remaining 90% of this, £9,000, to another customer. They lend it to Mrs Green who uses it to pay for a new kitchen from Mr White, who has a kitchen fitting business.*
- *Mr White takes the cheque and pays it into his bank. His bank can now lend 10% of £9,000 – £8,100 – to another customer. They lend this money to Mr Blue.*
- *Mr Blue spends this money on a new car, it is the import he has been waiting for six months.*
- *The agent in turn pays this money in their account at another bank who in turn can then lend £7,290.*
- *And so on . . .*

If the process is continued over a very large number of transactions, the total additional lending activity generated by the initial deposit of £10,000 is £90,000. This explains the concept of the *bank multiplier*, which is a numerical equation calculated as:

$$\text{Bank multiplier} = 1/\text{Reserve asset ratio}$$

In the above example bank multiplier = 1/10% = 10. In other words the total lending activity generated by the initial deposit, including the initial deposit itself is 10 times the initial deposit, i.e. £100,000.

3.6   So what determines whether interest rates are low or high? In the complex economies of today can be affected by a number of factors.

- **Inflation**: *as we have already seen when rates of inflation are high, interest rates tend to also be high for a number of reasons:*
  - *When savers see the value of their investments being eroded by inflation, financial services institutions have to pay higher rates of interest to attract new investment and retain existing funds.*
  - *When high inflation is increasing the cost of goods, people may decide to borrow in order to buy now before prices go up. This increases the demand for money, so the interest rate – the price of money – goes up. At the same time, the Bank of England may deliberately increase interest rates to discourage people from borrowing.*
- **Balance of payments**: *Interest rates tend to rise when there is a balance of payments deficit. This occurs when imports to a country exceed exports. There*

are two main reasons why a balance of payment deficit leads to higher interest rates:

- ○ *When imports (purchases) exceed exports (sales), there is a demand for money, which pushes up its price – the rate of interest.*
- ○ *The Bank of England may deliberately increase interest rates to reduce the attractiveness of borrowing money to purchase imported goods.*
- **World interest rates**: *If interest rates in other major trading nations are high, it may be necessary to keep UK interest rates high in order to discourage an outflow of funds. This outflow could cause a 'leakage' and reduce the money supply within the UK, which again has its own problems (see section 1.0).*

3.7 Although people sometimes refer to the rate of interest or to a market rate of interest, there is of course no single rate of interest in the economy. Different financial institutions, schemes or products offer a variety of interest rates, reflecting the individual characteristics of the products.

Note

What are the interest rates offered by your organisation on the different products available to customers?

What factors do you think affect the rates?

There are a number of factors that affect interest rates:

- Supply and demand: *interest has been defined as the price of money and, as with most things, the price is determined by supply and demand.*
- Risk: *higher-risk investment products (those linked to the stock market for example) usually offer a potentially higher rate of return. Simple deposit accounts where there is a negligible risk of losing the capital invested tend to offer the lowest rates of interest. Similarly, loans for speculative business ventures charge a higher rate of interest than mortgage loans for private house purchase.*
- Term: *as a general rule the longer the term (duration) the higher the rate of interest. If an investor is tying up money for, say five years, he or she will require a greater return than if the investment were only for one year.*

There can be an exception to that general rule, which may apply to institutions which buy-in funds at a fixed rate for onward lending to customers. They may do this rather than lend depositors' money (which they may not have access to) as in 3.5. If interest rates are expected to fall in the near future, longer-term rates could be lower than those offered for shorter periods.

- Amount: *larger investments tend to command higher rates of interest. Savings accounts often have a sliding scale of interest rates becoming progressively higher as more money is deposited.*

- Type of product: *different products are targeted at different customers and situations. For instance, to borrow £1,000 on credit card is usually more expensive than borrowing the same amount on an agreed overdraft.*

- Competition: *the financial market is highly competitive and institutions are always aware of the interest rates paid or charged by their competitors.*

- Profit: *As we have seen there is profit to be made by accepting deposits at a lower rate and lending funds at a higher rate.*

Think

Consider the following:

A financial services institution offers personal loans for cars and mortgages for house purchase. Which has the higher rate of interest and why?

3.8 We have looked at what factors affect interest rates and why these rates may move. To finish this topic area we should consider what the implications are for savers and borrowers when the interest rates move up and down.

Think

Think about these questions?

- *What happens to the interest a borrower receives on their deposit account when interest rates fall?*
- *What happens to the mortgage payments for a householder with a variable rate mortgage when interest rates rise?*

- *When interest rates fall, savers are worse off because their income decreases and borrowers are better off because their outgoings decrease.*

- *When interest rates rise, savers are better off because their income increases and borrowers are worse off because the outgoings increase.*
- *To help overcome this movement both savers and borrowers can use* fixed rate products *to make sure they know what money they will receive or pay out.*

Note

What fixed rate products does your organisation offer to help customers in this way?

4.0
State of the economy and public confidence

4.1   We have already said that the government seeks to pursue a number of economic and social objectives. Their exact aims may vary to some extent according to their political views, but the objectives generally include:

- *Reduction or elimination of unemployment.*
- *Stability of prices through low inflation.*
- *Steady growth of the economy.*
- *Increased standards of living.*
- *Acceptable foreign exchange rates.*
- *Stable balance of payments situation (imports and exports).*

The above objectives can be achieved through the application of monetary and fiscal policies. When trying to manage the economy the government has to consider both consumers and industry.

4.2   Consumers have their own concerns and will view the economy from the perspective of how it affects them and their family's finances. This will be in a number of ways, which are most likely to include some of the following:

- House prices – *this is considered to be a useful barometer of the health of the consumer side of the economy. People feel secure if the value of their house holds steady or increases. In the late 1980s and early 1990s house prices spiralled upwards, fuelled by people panic buying, and then crashed suddenly. Borrowers with mortgages were left with properties that were worth less than they had paid for them and in many cases with mortgages that were more than the value of the house. This* negative equity *situation caused financial hardship for such borrowers, as all their disposable income was needed to repay these loans. Not surprisingly consumer confidence was low at this time.*

- *Amount of disposable income – where there is confidence in housing and people have spare cash in their pockets, it fuels other parts of the economy. Consumers feel more willing to borrow and spend, so the volume of money in the money supply increases, as you would expect. Other factors here will include cheap interest rates, secure employment, low taxes and low inflation which keeps prices steady. It will also mean that consumers may be willing to save and spend money on financial services products which they may have considered a luxury when they had less spare cash.*

- *Value of sterling – when the value of the pound is high consumers can afford holidays aboard and foreign imports are cheap. This again will encourage people to spend but it doesn't mean that this is good for the economy as a whole if money is flowing out of the country as it reduces the money supply (see section 1.0).*

4.3   What is good for the consumer side of the economy is not always good for industry, in particular manufacturing. In simple terms:

- *The high value of sterling means that UK exports are expensive and uncompetitive abroad –*

- *This will lead to falling profits and ultimately failed businesses in the UK if the situation goes unchecked.*

4.4   So what can the Bank of England do to redress this issue? One action they can take is to raise interest rates. This is not likely to be popular for industry or consumers, however, it will have the effect of lowering the value of sterling abroad. This will have a two-fold effect:

- *it will decrease the volume of money in the money supply discouraging consumers from borrowing and spending. This will mean that less imported goods are bought and the end result will be that the value of sterling will decrease.*

- *this will lead to making UK exports less expensive and, therefore, more will be sold abroad, which will help industry. The catch is that UK manufacturers have to be able to afford the rise in interest rates in the short term.*

4.5   It can be seen that the consumer economy and the industrial economy appear to run at two different speeds. There will also be a time lag between any government intervention and the effects on the economy. It is a highly complex situation, much of which will depend on the collective view of consumers and their personal circumstances.

5.0
European union and monetary policy

5.1   There has been an increase in the profile and role of Europe on the UK for both consumers and industry. This has been down to successive British governments working more collaboratively with their European counterparts. This has led to a desire for European economic and monetary union. For financial services institutions it has led rise to such things as the threat of being acquired by a European bank and introduction of a new currency, the Euro.

5.2   First let us look at where the idea of European union came from. It was probably originally conceived by Sir Winston Churchill, who, in 1945, made an important speech on the theme of unity among European nations. This led to a number of treaties and the formation of the European Union. The name European Union (EU) has been introduced as an umbrella name of all the nations and the sub-organisations that are included.

5.3   The European Union is made up of 15 member countries with over 370 million citizens. The 15 member countries are as in Figure 1.4.

Founder members (1958)	West Germany (Germany was divided into East and West prior to 1989), France, Belgium, Netherlands, Luxembourg, Italy
1972	Great Britain, The Republic of Ireland, Denmark
1981	Greece
1986	Spain, Portugal
1995	Sweden, Finland

Figure 1.4 *The IS member countries of the European Union.*

It is the largest single trading block in the world. The EU is expected to increase in size in future years as applications have been received for another of other countries to join.

5.4   There are three main activities:

- *The executive is called the Council of Ministers, which members have authority to make policy on behalf of their own and other member states. The members are chosen representatives from the governments of their countries. The Council of Ministers has supreme influence over the policies of the EU in terms of decision-making ability. It meets mainly in Brussels.*
- *The principal forum for debate is the European Parliament, which usually sits in Strasbourg in France. It does not have the same responsibilities for the legislative*

process as parliament in Westminster and is more about implementation of European policies and managing its budget. Members of this Parliament (MEPs) are elected in their own country and do not have to be from the party that is in power in that country.

- The European Court of Justice and the European Court of First Instance are the two courts that make up the legal arm of the EU. Both courts are overseen by 15 judges, one from each member country; the courts sit in Luxembourg.

5.5 The broad objectives of the EU are as follows:

- A European single market – through dismantling of artificial trade barriers, the development of competition and regional policies.
- Economic and monetary union – macro-economic policy-making has been more co-ordinated and monetary union has moved closer with alignment of interest and inflation rates. Monetary union also implies the integration of the financial sectors of the union and the free movement of capital between the member states. This includes the fixing of exchange rates or the creation of a single currency.
- A European single currency – the Euro, more about this in section 5.8.

These objectives have so far had differing levels of success, however they remain goals, which can be aspired to.

5.6 So what does this all mean to the average European? For many people the European Council of Ministers and Parliament may seem very distant. The effects of European Union are somewhat ambiguous in that they depend on what appetite organisations and individuals have to integration. The benefits, a few of which are mentioned below, will take some time to reach the consumer:

- Reduced monopoly power, which means that organisations that have been used to a high degree of power at home will not continue to do so. The consumer should benefit from reduced prices as a result.
- Competition is likely to result in improved choice for consumers and greater inno-vation with more research and development. The removal of trade tariffs between EU countries also helps improve competition.
- Improved mobility of labour through such occurrences as the abolition of work permits and allowing the entitlement of social security benefits to be transferable between member states. Workers can choose to be taxed in their place of residence to avoid differences in income tax acting as a barrier to their movement. This is also where the minimum wage guidelines and maximum working hours per work-ing week have originated.
- The single currency will make movement between the EU countries much easier and negates the need to have a pocketful of different currencies. This will make

*business trips and holidays much easier and without the need to worry about fluc-
tuations in exchange rates and commission charges.*

These benefits, however, do not come without their issues and it could be argued
that there will be some areas that will benefit more than others, leaving some
parts of Europe with high unemployment. Despite the measures put in place,
labour is not as mobile as it could be, there are a number of barriers of which language
may be one.

5.7   For the UK financial service institution Europe and the single market concept
provides them with a number of issues.

- *There is already a high degree of competition within national markets with the
  consolidation of bank and building societies happening through acquisitions and
  mergers. The single market adds the threat of a takeover from outside the UK
  by a European bank (this has already happened with the examples from outside
  Europe such as Midland/HSBC and Yorkshire Bank/National Australia Bank).
  Consolidation alleviates some of the pressure of takeover and to a degree economies
  of scale should benefit customers as costs are reduced*

- *Cultural barriers such as language, as already mentioned, are also barriers to entry
  into foreign markets. Differences in legal and regulatory frameworks, and opening
  hours mean that the offices would have to be run very much in the local tradition
  rather than imposed by the parent company. Many countries have maintained some
  degree of protection over national institutions and nationalistic concerns still prevail.*

- *When looking at entering the European market, profit margins will be an area of
  concern. Interest rates are typically lower in mainland Europe when compared
  with the UK and home ownership is more unusual in these countries. Therefore,
  the opportunity to earn profit on lending funds to customers is less than in the UK
  and not an attractive market to become involved with. A number of UK banks
  have had offices in Europe and America in the past, however, these did not prove
  particularly profitable enterprises and were subsequently closed.*

- *There are some marked differences between banking in the UK and the rest of
  Europe. In some countries, e.g. Germany, Italy and Spain, banking is controlled
  or has its activities limited by government. Another difference in countries such as
  Spain, Italy, France and Germany is that they all operate substantial 'mutual' sectors
  (the organisations are similar to building societies in that the depositors are the
  owners). This is a significant barrier to UK banks entering the European market.*

- *There has been an increase in a trend towards banks working in partnership in
  areas such as bancassurance (provision of financial services that can fulfil both
  banking and insurance needs at the same time) and 'virtual banking' (banking
  via the Internet). This opens up more choice for customers and also greater
  innovation in the way that they can access products and services.*

5.8   The Euro

The introduction of the Euro has created a common denominator throughout Europe that can be used to measure and compare assets across borders. It has also given a common currency for payments between European countries. The implementation process has not been without its challenges:

- *The European Central Bank will have issued 14.5 billion bank notes worth 600 billion Euros by 1/1/2002.*
- *It has been estimated that the cost of preparation is between 2.5–3.5 times that of the cost of preparing for Y2K.*
- *Personal customers need more support and advice as they have had less information about the changes than business customers.*

Think

Think about this scenario

Imagine that you are visiting your favourite holiday resort in Spain but you haven't been to a 'Eurozone' country since the introduction of the new currency. What changes would you find?

- *Customers need to be familiar with what the new currency looks like and how they can obtain it.*
- *The country's old notes and coins cease to be legal tender at a future date. Not all these dates are the same for each country.*
- *The table below gives the currencies which have converted to the Euro and the Eurozone conversion rates: 1 Euro =*

Austrian schilling	13.8
Belgian franc	40.4
Dutch guilder	2.2
Finnish markkas	5.95
French franc	6.5
German mark	1.95
Greek drachma	340.7
Irish pound	0.8
Italian lire	1936
Luxembourg franc	40.4
Portuguese escudo	200.5
Spanish peseta	166

6.0
Major financial services institutions

Having looked at the big picture of the business environment in which financial services institutions exist, let us look in more detail at these organisations, the roles they play and what the differences are between them.

In the past, UK financial services organisations used to concentrate on a few specialised products and services. With deregulation and increased competition, organisations now offer a vast range of products and services. Even companies which do not have a financial services background, such as the supermarkets, have added these services to their product range to take advantage of the information they collect about customers and their needs.

6.1 The London market for banking and related products is enormous, companies from all over the world come to London-based institutions for financial services advice and expertise. The only realistic rivals to London are the markets in Tokyo, Frankfurt and New York. There are a number of factors that make the London market so important:

- **Tradition and track record**: *the UK was the first industrial power and was, therefore, the first to develop the financial systems needed to support this. Whilst this industrial strength is not so great today, the London financial services market still has a very high reputation.*
- **Specialisation**: *by specialising in particular financial products, City institutions have sharpened their competitive edge. The trend to diversify has not diminished the City's reputation for specialist services.*
- **Efficiency**: *deregulation has made the City more efficient and competitive. The UK financial system is one of the least restrictive in the world, while at the same time providing adequate and appropriate protection for investors.*
- **Geography**: *due to its location and the nature of world time zones, London markets have opening times that overlap the same trading day in both New York and Tokyo. With the advances in technology this has enabled 24-hour trading on the world's three major markets to become a reality.*

6.2 The London Stock Exchange
The London Stock Exchange is integral to the operation of the financial services system. It was established in 1773 as a market for buying and selling *securities*. It is still carrying out this function today, providing a market place through which buyers and sellers can trade shares, government securities, local authority stocks and foreign stocks. Buyers and sellers normally deal through intermediaries that are known as brokers, who are licensed by the Exchange. It also performs a

number of other functions that help to smooth the financial activities of commerce and government:

- **Raising capital:** *both government and industry can issue (sell) securities on the London Stock Exchange to raise new capital.*
- **Investor protection:** *the presence of a company's shares on the London Stock Exchange's official list implies that the company is believed to be profitable. If there is any doubt about the conduct of a company, permission to deal in that company's shares may be withdrawn.*
- **A measure of economic progress and prospects:** *the Stock Exchange publishes the progress of stocks and shares enabling investors to keep track of the value of their investments. Certain groups of these published prices are combined to give a general indication of the level of the market and the direction in which it is moving, e.g. Financial Times Ordinary Share Index and the FT-SE100 share Index.*

The London Stock Exchange used to be owned by its 'members', who were the individuals providing funding to buy and maintain the infrastructure. In 1986, after the 'Big Bang', the London Stock Exchange became a private limited company. In 2000 its shareholders voted to make the exchange a public limited company and it became the London Stock Exchange plc.

6.3 Retail financial services organisations

These types of institutions provide banking services that are commonly used by the general public and businesses. Typically these services will be current accounts, deposit accounts, loans and various insurance products. They are usually highly visible on the high street or through advertising on the Internet.

Note

Make a list of the major high street financial service organisations you are familiar with.

These financial organisations may also have other divisions, which can include mortgage provision, investment and corporate banking. This can be through subsidiaries or with partnerships with other financial organisations. The market is quite complex, particularly when some organisations appear to provide their own products but in fact they are using products supplied by another organisation. An example of this is the supermarket financial service providers who use an existing bank to supply the product.

Note

Make a list of those organisations which buy-in financial services from someone else to market under their own brand.

So, the question remains, what is a bank? It is basically a financial intermediary, which serves as a link between people and organisations with funds to deposit, and those who require funds in the form of loans (see section 3). The services are to help attract customers, thus attracting depositors and borrowers, which will also enable the on-selling of other products, which in turn will raise more revenue.

Not all of these institutions are 'clearing banks'. This term refers to the following process:

- *A clearing bank receives payments from other institutions in the form of cheques, direct debit and Switch transactions.*
- *The bank is due to make payments to these same institutions on behalf of its own customers who have issued cheques, direct debits and Switch transactions.*
- *The net effect is that each bank, at the end of each day's trading, is liable to pay or receive, a small balance from each of the other banks.*

The diagram in figure 1.5 illustrates how this might work in practice between two banks.

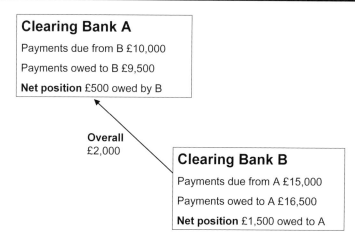

Figure 1.5 *Illustration of the settlement of clearing balances.*

Financial services institutions that do not have their own clearing service have to set up 'agency' arrangements with one of the clearing banks.

6.4   Merchant banks

Merchant banks are highly specialised and operate in the fields of corporate finance and investment management. They are often also involved in advising companies on the issuing of new share or loan capital. Merchant banks are not clearing banks and do not offer retail services. Many of the retail financial services institutions have merchant banking subsidiaries.

The types of services that merchant banks provide are include acceptance credits (short-term loan facilities), swaps and forward arrangements to cover the risk of from interest or currency fluctuations, treasury management and management of investment portfolios.

6.5   Finance houses

A finance house is basically a lending organisation. Rather than lending out deposits in the way that retail financial services organisations tend to, finance houses fund their operations mainly through the 'wholesale' finance market, 'buying' their money in. Some finance houses are independent, however, many are subsidiaries of larger groups. Examples of these would tend to be the financial organisations behind interest-free credit and loans available in most car showrooms, electrical and furniture stores. Their services are as follows:

- *Unsecured loans – usually between one and five years and for any purpose. Typically the rates of interest are higher than retail financial services providers as finance houses are prepared to accept greater risks.*

- *Secured loans – where a borrower is unable to obtain any more funding from their mortgage lender, the finance house may be prepared to lend instead. Again, this will carry a higher rate of interest and a 'second' charge will be registered behind the mortgage lender to provide security in the event of default.*

- *Hire purchase – this is the term given to buying items in instalments (primarily cars and household goods). The goods belong to the finance house until they are paid for and can legally be repossessed in the case of default.*

- *Leasing – the finance house retains ownership of the item, receives payments over a specified period and then takes back the item, selling it to recoup the outstanding value. The person leasing the item has the option of buying the item should they wish to at the end of the leasing period.*

- *Factoring – this is a service whereby the finance house manages the client company's invoices and debtors and collects the money owed to the company. In return for their services, the finance house retains a percentage of the debts collected as payment.*

Like all parts of the financial services industry the finance houses are keen to maintain a good image. Members of the Finance Houses Association subscribe to a voluntary code of practice aimed at maintaining and raising standards of responsible lending. They form an alternative choice for customers wishing to borrow funds.

6.6   Building societies

Building societies are mutual institutions, which are in effect owned by their members, who can determine how the organisation is managed. In the case of a building society the members comprise of the depositors and borrowers. The name stems from the 18th century when these organisations were set up to take in savings from the members and build houses, which were all occupied and eventually owned by the members. When all the members owned a home the society would be closed down.

These 'terminating' societies were later replaced by institutions that did not plan to terminate but kept on lending money for mortgage finance on an ongoing basis. These became known as 'permanent' building societies and this word can still be found in the names of some societies.

Up until recent times the building societies dominated the savings and mortgage market. In recent years, both the banks and building societies diversified their activities, until they have both become very similar. A number of building societies have 'de-mutualised' and with the consent of their members, turned into public limited companies. Some have resisted the pressure to convert believing that there are some distinct benefits retaining the 'mutual' status.

The possibility of a windfall on conversion to a public limited company has led to 'carpet-bagging'. This term refers to the practice of opening an account at a society that is believed to be going to convert, purely to obtain the allocation of shares. Societies, which are concerned about protecting the interests of their long-term members, place restrictions on opening new accounts or to whom the shares in the new company will be available.

Think

Consider this scenario

> You have a building society account that qualifies for shares in the proposed new company. What might the advantages and disadvantages be of converting to a public limited company?

6.7   Government savings schemes – National Savings and Gilt-edged stocks
When government expenditure exceeds income from tax and national insurance contributions the government has to borrow to make up the difference. This difference is known as the public sector borrowing requirement (PSBR). There are three main ways it can do this:

- **Treasury bills**: *short-term loans to the government which are traded on the discount market on the London Stock Exchange.*
- **Gilt-edged stocks (gilts)**: *These are long-term loans to the government, which can be as long as 30 years or in some cases with no specified end date. Both these and Treasury bills are low risk forms of investment for investors as they are backed by the government.*
- **National Savings**: *This is the government's primary source of borrowing from individuals through a wide range of savings and investment products. They can be bought are the Post Office or directly from National Savings headquarters. There are a variety of deposit accounts and bonds, some which have tax advantages to make them more attractive to savers.*

Think

> Next time you visit the Post Office pick up a few of the leaflets about National Savings and compare them to other products offered by the financial services institutions.

6.8   Insurance organisations
Insurance organisations cover a wide range of products and services. They can be either purely insurance related or connected to another financial service provider.

Primarily there are two main areas of insurance activity:

- *Life assurance – payment of benefits dependent upon circumstances related to the death or survival of a person or persons. This can also include policies relating to sickness or accident. These fall into two further categories:*
  - *Protection products – to provide for individuals (or businesses) should they suffer adverse financial effects due to death or illness.*
  - *Savings products – to provide a lump sum at the end of a term of regular saving. Such policies are known as endowment assurance.*
- *General insurance – insurance against the loss of, or damage to, property. Typically this may be car, home and contents or holiday insurance.*

Many of the large insurance companies also provide the following products and services:

- *Pension funds – receiving contributions from people who are working and who wish to set aside funds to provide for their old age. Since it is not unusual for people to live as long as 30 years after their retirement, it is important that they make adequate provision to maintain the standard of living when they do so. It is generally accepted that the state pension benefits are barely adequate to achieve this and increasingly so in the future as the trend is towards an ageing population. There are a number of different schemes available to meet the needs of most customers.*
- *Unit trusts – this is the term given to 'pooled' investments, which enable the smaller investor to invest on the stock market in an efficient manner. Along with many other investors they contribute to a large fund either by lump sum or regular saving. They can take the advantage of having a professional fund manager, spreading the risk over a large number of stocks and shares and can advantage of reduced investment charges than if they were investing their money directly.*

6.9   Other financial institutions

- *Investment trusts – these appear to be similar to unit trusts and operate in a similar way. However, these are not 'trusts' but are limited companies whose business it is to make profits by investing in the stocks and shares of other companies. They issue a fixed number of shares and are not, therefore, open-ended funds.*
- *Centralised mortgage lenders – they were established in the 1980's as mortgage providers funded by the wholesale market.*
- *Credit unions – these are small, often local, organisations that receive regular savings from personal customers and then grant small loans (e.g. for household goods or holidays) based on a multiple of the savings accumulated.*

7.0
Meeting customer needs

Let's now consider the different customer needs and how these organisations can meet these needs. There is a vast amount of choice available to customers. The organisations and individuals who are employed by them can take an active role in helping customers make those important choices about their financial well-being. Done effectively this can be a way of aiding organisations differentiate themselves from the competition.

By way of introduction the UK economy can be thought of as being made up of four main sectors:

- *Personal.*
- *Public.*
- *Company.*
- *Overseas.*

This section deals with the personal sector. Whilst the personal sector includes the affairs of unincorporated businesses, private trusts, and some non-profit making bodies such as charities and clubs, this section will concentrate on the matters affecting individuals and their immediate households.

7.1 To help us understand the concept of customer needs, let us consider the idea of personal assets. Personal funds that are not spent immediately or within a very short time can be used to build up personal wealth. The personal sector derives its funds from four main areas:

- *Wages, salaries and profits from self-employment, which form the bulk of personal sector income.*
- *Transfers of income from central or local government, such as state pensions and social security benefits.*
- *Withdrawals from savings, including interest and other income from investments.*
- *Borrowing.*

The ways in which this personal wealth is held falls into two categories:

- *Physical assets: these are things of value; such as land a house or a car. The majority of this form of wealth is held in private dwellings.*
- *Financial assets: these are the forms of wealth held in financial institutions, such as deposit accounts, unit trusts and pension plans. There are a broad range of products with varying amounts of liquidity, risk, growth and income.*

7.2 There is a well-established pattern in the way in which most savers and investors hold their assets. It begins with liquidity and safety and then moves away from liquidity and towards greater risk.

Figure 1.6 shows examples of products that would fulfil this hierarchy of needs. Individuals tend not to move onto the next stage of liquidity and risk until their needs have been met at the existing level. So for the first stage of cash, individuals would not start saving until they have sufficient funds to meet their day-to-day requirements. At the top of the needs hierarchy are the types of products such as unit trusts or shares, which offer greater potential over the long-term but at the risk of short-term loss.

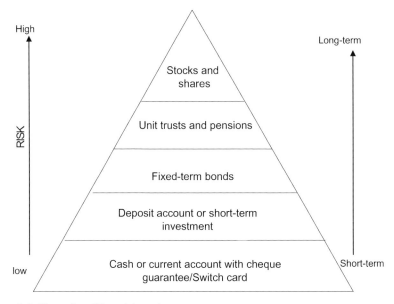

Figure 1.6 *Hierarchy of financial needs.*

Think

Consider this:

Plot your own position on the hierarchy of needs triangle.

7.3   There are lots of ways of segmenting needs by organisations for marketing and sales activity. One way is by age or *life-stages*. It is well established that the financial needs of individuals and families change and develop as people pass though the different stages of life. While accepting that everyone is different, there are some broad statements that can be made.

- **School age young people**: *it is typical for accounts to be opened for young people by their grandparents or other relatives, at birth or later for birthday gifts. They may be attracted by small-lump sum or regular savings scheme bonuses or perhaps with incentives such as free moneyboxes or other gifts.*

  Retail financial service providers and building societies offer such accounts and National savings are also popular as it is possible to obtain tax free interest up to a certain limit. Stakeholder pensions may also prove a popular savings vehicle as contributions do not require earned income.

- **Teenager and students**: *at this stage few young people have any surplus income, although some who have started full-time or holiday work will require current account facilities and may be able to accumulate some savings.*

  Some may borrow to purchase a car or fund a holiday. Many students have to borrow to supplement grants, mainly through special schemes established for that purpose.

- **Post-education young people**: *The ability to save increases for those in employment, with the possibility of higher incomes as careers progress. If they establish a home of their own (often by renting first) their savings initially will be modest.*

  It is more likely that they will need to borrow, so their ability to afford other products such as insurance will be limited. It is unlikely that they will have dependents who would be financially at risk should anything happen to them.

- **Young families**: *although fewer young people today get married, many still form relationships and raise families. This often leads to increased borrowing, particularly for a mortgage. At the same time income may be reduced if one partner gives up work to look after children, so again there is little scope for savings.*

  Protection of the earners' income against illness or death becomes very important because of the dependent children. Young families should also think about pension provision, although it is likely that very few do.

- **Established families**: *as families settle into an established lifestyle, they tend to become better off financially. There may be a return to a two-income situation. Many people trade up to a larger house, increasing their borrowing accordingly. Their creditworthiness may improve, enabling greater borrowing capacity for cars and household goods.*

  This is also the time when wealth may be increased by the receipt of inheritances from the estates of parents or other relatives.

- **Mature households**: *this is generally the period of highest earning potential and outgoings may also decrease as children leave home and mortgages are paid off.*

  Pension provision becomes a priority, with many people realising that they are not going to have as high an income in retirement as they had hoped.

- **Retirement**: *prior to retirement most people's financial planning is centred on converting income into lump-sums (or lump-sums into bigger lump-sums). At retirement, when income from employment ceases, the focus changes, the requirement is now to produce income from capital.*

  The need to prepare for possible inheritance tax liabilities should also be considered. The cost of health care and possibly long-term care in old age are further issues.

7.4   So far we have established how wealth is accumulated and stored by individuals and how, over time and changing circumstances, their needs change. The mainstream financial products that meet these needs will be dealt with in the next module – Unit 2. Let us now consider how the different organisations reach their customers and what they can do to help customers make choices about the financial products they buy.

Until the 1970s at least, it had been taken for almost for granted that financial services were only of interest to a certain type of person. This person was characterised in a lot of financial marketing as being over 25, serious minded seeking security and reliability above all.

Over the last 20 years, providers of financial services, like the providers of many other goods and services, have discovered that their products can be successfully and profitably marketed to whole new segments of the population. In particular they have learned that younger people are earning significant salaries and can be attracted to financial services by advertising and by the provision of products that meet the needs of their particular lifestyles. Internet and telephone banking and 24-hour availability of cash are examples.

Such developments are part of the process by which marketing departments continually review the composition of the potential customer base and aim to match a suitable mix of products to the market segments identified in their strategic plan. Supermarkets collect information in the customer loyalty schemes, which can be used to inform them about a customer's buying habits and therefore their likely financial requirements. For example, a customer suddenly buying baby products could be direct mailed information about how to provide for the new arrival's future.

7.5   Deregulation of banks and building societies in the 1980s and 1990s has meant that there are more institutions offering a wider variety of products and services. This has led to fierce competition, which has generally resulted in a better deal for the customer both in terms of service and price. It does mean however that organisations have to work harder to create and keep a customer. Customers in turn are becoming better informed and more demanding in their expectations. It has also meant a squeeze on profits, which has led financial services organisations to search for more cost-effective procedures and the advances in technology have made alternative ways of interacting with customers available.

This has led to a need for organisations to differentiate themselves against the competition. This can be done in a number of ways:

- *Advertising and marketing campaigns, e.g. Barclays and the appeal of a 'big bank'.*
- *Overt policy, e.g. co-operative and ethical trading.*
- *Matching delivery mechanism to target segment, e.g. Egg and Virgin Direct for Internet banking for the busy professional.*
- *Type of product, e.g. Woolwich open plan combined mortgage and current account.*
- *Relationship management, e.g. NatWest and the personal banking manager.*

7.6   The way in which financial services organisations reach their customers has also changed. The traditional way for banks and building societies to reach their customers was via the 'high street' branch. These networks have been downsized, the main offices being in cities and larger towns. The branch provides the best way of meeting on a face-to-face basis or where some sort of ongoing relationship is required.

The marketing functions of these branches have been centralised and transferred, to some extent, to direct mail. Improved marketing can help customers make choices about products. This can take a variety of forms through the media, PR and advertising, direct mailing (this can yield profitable results if correctly planned and managed, but tends to suffer from the 'junk mail' image) and newsletters.

Banking transactions, particularly cash withdrawals have been taken over by Automated Teller Machines (ATMs). These machines are increasingly located in places where there is no branch presence.

Note

Make a list of the places where you have noticed or used ATMs.

The ATM technology is expensive to install but in the longer term costs fall due to the ability to deal with large volumes of business.

7.7   Insurance companies have been steadily reducing their branch networks too and now most retain offices only in major cities. They operate mainly through independent financial advisers, tied agents or their own direct salesforce. Large retail financial institutions that do not have their own insurance arm can chose to work in partnership with an insurance company and in effect become a 'tied' agent. These sales people are required to give advice on 'regulated products' (see Unit 2) and to make recommendations on information collected from the customer about their lifestyle and needs.

7.8   Telephone call centres have been the way that many organisations have been able to reach the largest number of their customers to give service and sales advice. Customers can obtain all the usual banking services at their own convenience, rather than having to visit a branch with set opening hours. Employees work flexible hours to enable this service to be operated. Because of this shift pattern, customers aren't always able to speak to the same member of staff, which means there is a need for good record keeping of conversations and transactions.

Think

Think about this:

> How can you make up for that fact that although your customers may be longstanding, you may not have spoken to them before?

7.9   Online banking, via the Internet, is fast becoming a new delivery medium backed up by the 'contact' centre operation. Customers can obtain account balances, transfer money, set up and cancel standing orders and buy products in this way. This can, therefore, be more convenient and quicker than a contact centre. However, it is more difficult for customers to obtain advice using this medium for those that know what they want, it is an excellent method for routine transactions. Given that the Financial Services Act requires financial services institution to 'know your customer' this may restrict the extent to which services can be sold over the Internet and advice can be given.

7.10   There is a need for all staff talking to customers, whether face-to-face or on the telephone, to be able to build rapport, ask questions, to listen and then be able to provide information that will help the customer make a decision. This is the distinct advantage that human contact has over technology. Services are often tiered by cost. Mass market is free to all, relationship managed customers carry a charge and those with significant wealth tend to receive a different type of service altogether. This range of choice however, can exclude those on a very low income or those people who deal on a cash only system.

Customers have an enormous array of choices to suit their lifestage and lifestyle needs and depending upon their particular circumstances staff members can help them chose which product or service will be right for them. By collecting information about the customer financial service providers are able to create innovative new solutions, such as the flexible mortgage and 'one-stop' accounts to attract and retain new customers.

8.0
Social responsibility and ethics

8.1   Given that there is a high degree of competition in the financial services market and a constant drive to create and retain customers, organisations and the individuals employed by them need to adhere to codes of conduct that befit the corporate image of the company and the expectations of society at large, as to how that company will behave. It is expected that a large organisation will make some contribution to society and that it will act in a way that is not irresponsible or harmful to the general public.

Research has shown that there is an increasing view within the UK that a business should be considering the needs of the community in which it operates. There is also evidence that potential customers do consider a company's record in matters of social responsibility when deciding if they want to do business with them. There may, therefore be an effect on the profits of the business if the company does not take this matter seriously.

The company has a 'stakeholder' responsibility to all those people that are part of it in some way. This involves employees, suppliers, distributors and customers. This means that the company should always consider its actions to ensure that these groups of people are not harmed in any way.

8.2   Linked to this is the idea of ethics. Generally ethics is a term used to distinguish what is morally right from what is morally wrong. While a great deal of the financial services industry is highly regulated, the rules and regulations deal with those clear rules which can actually be enforced. Ethical issues are generally not covered by regulation. Although it is true that some unethical activity would also be illegal, there is a great deal of behaviour, which, while legal, would still be considered to be against ordinary decency. A business has to make judgments everyday and needs to consider ways in which these are made, asking itself if these decisions would be judged to be either ethical by members of the public. Managers and team members need to continually assess what they are doing to ensure that they do not do anything that would violate ordinary decency or promote or condone such behaviour.

Whilst it may seem that at first glance that the financial services arena may escape such problematic decisions this is not the case. There are still a great number of issues that could have ethical implications.

Think

Consider the following:

> Ethical dilemma No. 1 – What level of profit is it acceptable to make from the public?
> *Financial services institutions could well be accused of unethical behaviour in their profit margins. These organisations can make huge profits, yet each year hundreds of small businesses fold and many more struggles with cash flow problems. This is legal but is it ethical?*
>
> Ethical dilemma No. 2 – Financial advisors are expected to give their customers the best advice for their needs. Should they be paid commission for making sales?
> *Some people would argue that if financial advisers are paid to make sales that they might be tempted to sell those products even if the customer doesn't really need them.*
>
> Ethical dilemma No. 3 – A product/service is re-priced at a cheaper rate to attract new customers. Should this new price be offered to existing customers?
> *If this lower price is not offered to those customers who have previously bought the service and shown loyalty to the company is it ethically correct?*

These kinds of issues will face managers and team members every day and they will need to ensure that the decisions they take are carefully thought out. These decisions need to be based on the following factors, they should:

- *Reflect their professionalism and their ethics, i.e. they should never take decisions that will knowingly harm people.*
- *Where possible, be honest and fair to all parties including new and existing customers, employees, the public and the company.*
- *Avoid false or misleading claims about the products and services they offer.*
- *Disclose the full cost of the product or service to the buyer.*
- *Not exploit the customer's needs or their expertise in the marketing and selling process.*
- *Not exert undue pressure on staff to sell particular products.*

8.3   The company has 'societal' responsibility that relates to the organisation's responsibility and its attitude to the general public. This kind of responsibility would manifest itself in such things as the organisation supporting ecological matters and supporting environmentally friendly products.

Many financial services organisations are a significant part of the community in which they operate. They may well employ a large proportion of the workforce in a particular area and may well be responsible for its financial stability.

8.4   Most financial services organisations are very conscious of their responsibilities to staff and in order to create an image of social responsibility at stakeholder level, they will endeavour to show support for staff and their families. This may be in the form of sport and leisure facilities or even a crèche to allow parents to return to work more easily. It could be argued that these are simply perks to attract and retain good quality people and, therefore, the company does it for commercial reasons. This may be the case however, it is likely to attract more staff, as they are perceived as a caring employer.

At societal level the company can create an image of social responsibility by supporting good causes, making donations and sponsorships. While this will obviously carry a cost the benefits are great in terms of their image and there could be a commercial benefit as a result of the company's socially responsible attitude. This can be linked to the use of a credit card that has been issued on behalf of a charity or having company literature printed on recycled paper.

Note

Find out what your company is doing to promote an image of social responsibility.

Unit 2

Describe the mainstream types of personal financial services products

The aim of this module is to enable you to:

- *Explain the differences between regulated and non-regulated products.*
- *Describe what regulated products are.*
- *Describe what non-regulated products are.*
- *Outline other intermediaries who provide advice for customers.*

One of the objectives pursued by modern governments is the establishment of a stable economic environment (as we have seen in Unit 1). This environment needs to balance the need for businesses to make a profit with the right of consumers to receive a fair deal. This has led to the regulation, in varying degrees, of many industries in the UK.

As money is a vital denominator in both the lives of individuals and the national economy, the financial services industry has become perhaps the most regulated business sector of all. Although government tries to foresee problems and to introduce legislation as 'prevention rather than cure', it remains true that much regulatory legislation is reactive rather than proactive. It may be the result of particular scandals or crises, or simply in response to changes in lifestyles, in business methods and in products.

This section of the study text deals with the mainstream types of financial services products and their provision to the personal customer. These products are known as either 'regulated' or 'non-regulated' under the terms of the Financial Services and Markets Act 2000 (FSMA), which has replaced the Financial Services Act 1986 and other related legislation. The FSMA itself and the other types of legislation that are applicable to financial products are covered in detail in Unit 4.

1.0
Differences between regulated products and non-regulated products

1.1   Main differences between regulated and non-regulated products

The regulatory requirements are laid down in the Financial Services and Markets Act 2000 ('FSMA' or 'the Act'). As you will see further in Unit 4, the Act lays down strict rules governing the treatment of investment business including who can carry out such business, how it is carried out and how complaints are handled.

So that you can understand these rules it is important to know what is meant by the term 'investment'. This was originally defined by the Financial Services Act 1986 in which investments are defined as where:

- *The capital is at risk.*
- *There is a contract or certificate.*
- *The purpose is to make a gain.*

Note

What financial services products might fulfil these criteria?

Such products that fulfil these criteria are:

- *Shares.*
- *Unit trusts and open ended investments.*
- *Personal pensions.*
- *Life assurance.*
- *Government securities (gilt-edged stock).*

> **Note**
>
> What financial service products would not fulfil these criteria?

Such products that do not fulfil these criteria are:

- *Current/cheque accounts.*
- *Deposit/savings accounts.*
- *Loans.*
- *Credit cards.*
- *General insurance products such as car insurance.*

On this basis, conducting investment business includes:

- *Arranging deals in investments.*
- *Giving advice on investments.*

On a statutory basis (by law), therefore, these are the types of regulated and non-regulated products. With the Financial Services Authority (FSA) becoming the single regulator of the financial services industry (see Unit 4 for more details) there are other types of products and services which it will have control over in the future.

One such example is mortgage providers and mortgages. It could be said that the FSA already regulates some mortgage providers, in the sense that it has had regulatory responsibility for banks for some time. From November 2001 it regulated the other main mortgage providers, the building societies, when it took over the responsibilities of the Building Societies Commission.

Specific regulation of mortgage provision has in fact been in place for a while on a 'self-regulatory' basis, through the Code of Mortgage Lending Practice, now known as the Mortgage Code. Although it is a voluntary code, almost all lenders subscribe to it.

The Code has been in force for lenders since July 1999. Although it is voluntary for intermediaries too, most do subscribe to it, because subscribing lenders will not accept business from intermediaries who do not subscribe.

Compliance with the Mortgage Code is monitored by a body known as the Mortgage Board (formerly the Mortgage Code Compliance Board). The Mortgage Board will continue to oversee this important area of non-statutory regulation.

Organisations which are registered with the Mortgage Board are required to meet certain 'fit and proper' criteria in relation to senior staff, controllers and supervisors. These criteria are similar to those which will apply under FSA regulation and in order to avoid duplication of administration, FSA-authorised firms will normally be exempt from meeting these Mortgage Board requirements.

The FSA will take steps towards an appropriate involvement in the regulation of the mortgage industry. One of the FSA's main aims, of its rules for this industry, is to ensure that a more balanced approach is adopted to the giving of information to customers – in particular features which might be considered to be the more negative aspects of mortgage deals, such as redemption penalties and compulsory insurances, which should be given more prominence in advertisements. In addition, customers will have to be given a 'pre-application illustration' which must also give prominence to these factors.

These rules will cover only lenders and will not relate directly to intermediaries. However, lenders will be required to take reasonable steps to ensure that intermediaries do provide customers with these illustrations. It is expected that they will apply from a date around July 2002.

So it can be seen that, although not regulated by law, mortgage products and services will be regulated by the FSA on a voluntary basis through the Mortgage Code. It could well be that other areas of the financial services industry, such as general insurance, may follow at a later date.

1.2   Sources of regulation – prior to the 1980s, regulation of the financial services industry in the UK was a rather piecemeal affair, with a number of different bodies operating under the terms of a wide range of laws and regulations, many of which were seriously out of touch with the demands of a fast-moving and fast-changing industry. This situation was rectified to some extent by the passing of a number of significant items of legislation:

- *The Banking Act 1979 introduced a legal definition of what constituted a bank and introduced protection of depositors' money through supervision of banks.*
- *The Financial Services Act 1986 introduced a more coherent system of regulation for investment products, establishing a range of regulations to be policed by a self-regulatory environment overseen by the Securities and Investments Board (SIB).*

- *The Building Societies Acts of 1986 and 1997 expanded the powers of building societies, enabling them to offer many more of the services, which were previously the province of banks and other financial service providers.*
- *The Banking Act 1987 built on the 1979 Act and formalised several features of regulation.*

By the mid-1990s it was felt that the system was still too fragmented for the increasingly integrated world of financial services in the UK. In addition, several prominent incidents – notably the Maxwell affair and the collapse of Barings Bank – led to the view that a single, more powerful, regulator was required.

The Chancellor of the Exchequer, therefore, announced in May 1997 that financial services regulation in the UK would be reformed again, under the auspices of a new single regulator, the Financial Services Authority (FSA).

2.0
Why is regulation necessary?

In the past, as the amount of regulation has increased due to failures and shortcomings within the financial services industry, so the amount of statutory measures increased. Due to a number of scandals, financial losses, instances of mis-selling, claims of overcharging and of poor service, the public began to lose confidence in the financial services sector and many financial services organisations gained a poor reputation in the media. There was a growing need to ensure high standards right across the industry. The government, therefore, stepped in to ensure that customers are protected in the safest possible way through legislation and regulation.

Think

What are some of the financial services scandals that you can recall?

When the newly-elected Labour administration took over in 1997 there were five areas of regulation – deposit taking, insurance, securities and corporate finance, fund management and retail investment advice.

This had led to a number of bodies that carried out regulatory activities, in many cases, acting independently of each other. As financial services organisations typically undertook activities in a number of the five areas, this caused duplication for the banks, and customers to be unsure who they could approach for help if they had a complaint which could not be settled with the organisation itself. For instance an ordinary current account customer potentially would have to approach a different body for a complaint about a deposit account, an insurance product, a share deal and advice about an investment product. A new regulator, which covered all these areas, would be able to do so more economically and efficiently and so provide a better service to customers and the financial services organisations themselves.

The main objective of the Financial Services Authority (FSA) is to secure the appropriate degree of protection for consumers. In this, particular attention is given to the differing degree of risk associated with the vast array of investment products and the differing degrees of experience and expertise that different consumers may have with the breadth of regulatory activity.

The FSA has the following statutory objectives:

- *Maintaining confidence in the UK financial system.*
- *Promoting public understanding of the financial system (including public awareness of the benefits and risks of different forms of financial transactions).*
- *Securing an appropriate level of protection for consumers. An 'appropriate' level may depend on:*
  - *The different level of risk that relates to different investments.*
  - *The different experience/expertise of different consumers.*
  - *The consumers' need for accurate advice and information.*
  - *The principle that consumers should take responsibility for their decisions.*
- *Contributing to the reduction of financial crime. The three main areas of financial crime which the FSA seeks to control are:*
  - *Money laundering.*
  - *Fraud and dishonesty, including e-crime.*
  - *Criminal market conduct such as insider dealing.*

The FSA, as well as scrutinising organisations and looking at the financial services industry as a whole, will undertake assessments across 'sectors'. It may decide, for example, to undertake a risk-assessment exercise with all organisations selling with-profits-based products or certain types of equity products. This is what the FSA has termed a 'theme-based' approach to risk assessment. This is one of the innovative features of the new regime and allows the FSA to be proactive rather than reactive in highlighting and investigating problems.

Some recent themes have been about:

- *Gauging levels of consumer awareness to with-profits products following the failure of some endowment policies linked to mortgages. The aim was to try to ascertain whether more information needs to be disclosed to customers and if there is enough consumer protection when products are sold.*

- *General disclosure of information – investigating whether information disclosed to the regulator also be disclosed to the general public.*

Other themes identified have been:

- *Money laundering.*
- *E-Commerce.*
- *The implications of a low-inflation economy.*

The FSA will deploy its resources, skills and attention where it thinks the greatest financial risks are likely to occur. Large organisations will have quite a close relationship with the FSA and its supervisors and the impact of any failings will be quite severe.

There is, therefore, a new operating framework designed to identify the main risks to the FSA's statutory objective as they arise and to help plan how to address these risks.

The diagram in Figure 2.1 shows the process of identifying risks to the statutory objectives, assessing and prioritising the risks and deciding the appropriate regulatory response, using a range of regulatory tools.

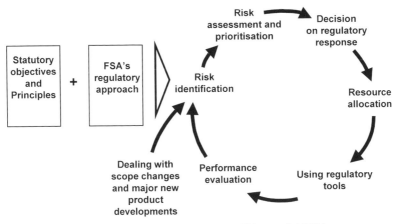

Figure 2.1 *The FSA's new operating framework – from FSA material 2001.*

2.1 Benefits of regulation by the FSA to the financial services organisation – there are a number of benefits of having the new regulator to financial services organisation:

- *Financial services organisations cease to be troubled by the issue of which regulator should deal with which part of their business.*

- *There are common rules of engagement that all providers need to adhere to, ensuring that no one organisation has an unfair advantage.*
- *Having authorised status shows customers that the organisation is reputable in the marketplace and that it meets the standards laid down. This should help to improve customer confidence in the organisation, its staff and its products.*
- *Proactive risk assessment of various sectors of industry should highlight any problems in their early stages which will help to support the public's confidence in the financial services sector.*

2.2   A customer under the FSMA is defined as a person 'who is using or may be contemplating using any of the services provided by the authorised person' (organisation). This means that a customer doesn't have to have bought a product to take advantage of the rights afforded them under the FSA rulings. There are some distinct benefits to the customer of having these rules in place. These are:

- *Customers receive all the necessary information they need to make a decision, which means that they understand the transaction and feel in control. This will give them increased peace of mind.*
- *They are aware of the upsides and downsides of any investment and understand the risks associated with it. They should be able to make the best choice for their individual needs and circumstances. This ensures the suitability of the product they are considering.*
- *Illustrations will provide an indication of anticipated performance, however, any negative aspects of the product will be clearly outlined, again giving peace of mind.*
- *If a customer has a complaint there will be clear guidelines of how they can get this resolved. If they feel their complaint has not been resolved satisfactorily by the financial service provider then they have one point of contact to take the matter forward with an independent external body. There is a consumer help line for customers to contact with any queries from checking the authorisation status of an organisation to information about financial planning advice.*

2.3   The FSA has produced an enforcement manual designed to provide guidance for 'authorised' and 'non-authorised' persons and organisations (see section 3 for further details of these terms). The regulator has the power to bring criminal proceedings for cases of insider dealing, misleading statements and practical offences as well as to issue financial penalties for market abuse. These penalties are designed to maintain confidence in the UK financial system. The FSA's enforcement powers are extremely strong. They include the right to prosecute and impose unlimited fines and banishment orders. Any enforcement decision that an organisation or individual does not agree with can be heard afresh by the Financial Services and Markets

Tribunal. This gives an independent assessment of the case and the proposed penalties.

The following are the areas that the FSA's enforcement manual covers:

- *Information and powers of investigation – the FSA may request, in writing specific information and documents within a specified timescale. It may also require individuals involved in the investigation to attend meetings to answer questions.*
- *Injunctions – the FSA has the power to apply for an injunction against persons who contravene a relevant requirement. It also has asset freezing powers.*
- *Withdrawal of approval – it can prevent people not deemed fit and proper from performing 'controlling' functions. In this decision the FSA will consider the person's previous disciplinary actions and general compliance history.*
- *Prohibition of individuals – in very serious cases the FSA has the power to prohibit an approved person from carrying out regulated activities. People prohibited from carrying out regulated activities will be entered on to the FSA register and organisations have an obligation to check that they are not employing prohibited persons.*
- *Insolvency proceedings and orders against debt avoidance – the aim of this enforcement action is to stop organisations or persons from carrying on business while insolvent and to ensure the orderly restitution and distribution of assets.*
- *Discipline of firms and approved persons – the FSA may decide to issue a private warning instead of formal disciplinary action. It has a number of criteria which helps it to make this decision.*
- *Sanctions for market abuse – The regulator aims to protect prescribed markets from any damage to efficiency caused by the manipulation or misuse of information. The FSA has the power to bring about criminal prosecutions for insider dealing or the issuing of misleading statements. It also has the power to impose financial penalties, publish statements or obtain injunctions in cases of market abuse.*
- *Prosecution of criminal offences – the FSA has the power to prosecute in cases where there is evidence of:*
  - *individuals carrying out regulated activity without authorisation – this means that a person giving a customer investment advice when he is not authorised to do so will have some serious implications for that person;*
  - *making false claims that a person is authorised;*
  - *misleading the FSA;*
  - *performing functions in breach of a prohibition order;*
  - *offering new securities to the public before issuing a prospectus;*
  - *failing to co-operate with the FSA; or*
  - *failing to comply with provisions about control over authorised persons.*

- *Disqualification of auditors and actuaries – auditors and actuaries hold an important position in relation to financial services organisations and the FSA has the power to disqualify those that fail to maintain the appropriate standards and publish this in its register.*
- *Disapplication orders against members of the profession – the FSA has the power to disqualify auditors and actuaries from acting for specific organisations, unit trust schemes or open-ended investment companies if they are found to be in breach of the trust rules.*

You can see from the above that there are some quite serious penalties that can be imposed. Everyone working in the financial services environment has a duty of care to follow the guidelines laid down by the regulator and their employer, to protect themselves and their customers from any unnecessary risk. If you are not an authorised adviser then you must not give advice or make recommendations or ask questions which may be construed as such.

Note

If you are not an authorised advisor:

What types of questions should you **not** ask customers?

What sorts of statements should you **not** make to customers?

The types of questions you should **not** ask customers are:

- *How do you feel about risk?*
- *What plans do you have for that money?*
- *What are the charges like for that service?*
- *Do you contribute to a personal pension plan?*

The types of statements should you **not** make to customers?

- *I think you should do this, you can clearly afford to.*
- *This product is right for you.*
- *This product has always done well.*

Note

If you are not an authorised advisor:

What types of questions could you ask customers?

What sorts of statements could you make to customers?

The types of questions you **can** ask are:

- *Can you tell me if you have any investments?*
- *Can you tell me how much you have invested already?*
- *When do you plan to retire?*
- *How would you feel about talking to my colleague about this?*

The types of statements you could make to customers are:

- *Our products are from the Marketing Group of . . .*
- *Our advisers are tied to our company.*

The next section explains who can sell regulated products (an authorised person), the concept of best advice and what you can do if you are not authorised to sell regulated products.

3.0
Regulated products

3.1   Before exploring the concept of authorised and non-authorised sellers let us first take a look at what is meant by an authorised organisation or in the language of the regulations an authorised 'firm'.

Organisations must be 'authorised' to carry on regulated activity and this means they must fulfil certain criteria and adhere to the standards laid down. Certain organisations such as the London Stock Exchange or the Bank of England are considered to be 'exempt' from needing to obtain such authorisation. There is also the effect of 'polarisation'. Polarisation was brought about by the Financial Services Act 1986 and relates to 'packaged' products (i.e. life assurance, pensions and unit trusts etc.). It meant that a clear distinction has been made between:

- *those people that only sell products of one company (or marketing group) who are known as tied advisers (or company representatives); and*
- *those people who sell products from the whole market place who are called Independent Financial Advisors.*

Note

How does your organisation stand in terms of polarisation?

Does your company employ tied or independent financial advisers?

Organisations had to chose which route they were going to take when this law was enacted. The choice was to have their own tied advisors selling their own products or to have independent advisors selling the products of other companies or in some cases to have a separate division doing each activity.

3.2   Tied advisers:
- are agents of the company they work for and are usually employees of the tied agents or a member of a marketing group (e.g. The retail arm of a bank may belong to the Marketing Group offering insurance, share-dealing and other investment products). They can be self-employed advisers who chose to tie themselves to the products of one company;
- can only advise or sell products provided by a particular company or group of companies;
- are authorised by the company they work for and that company is responsible for ensuring compliance with the rules laid down by the FSA;
- when advising customers, if they do not have a suitable product from within their own company's Marketing Group's product range, they must inform their customer. They may in this case refer the customer on to an independent adviser; and
- are authorised through the company or firm to which they are tied. The authorised firm then accepts responsibility for its tied representatives.

3.3   Independent advisors:
- are not tied to any particular company and can recommend investments from a wide range of providers;
- must act in the best interests of their clients at all times whilst ensuring their own interests do not prejudice the advice they give;
- advice must not be influenced by the amount of commission they are to receive by selling a particular product;
- must be able to identify more than one product provider so that the customer has a choice, to select the most suitable provider of a regulated product by considering a range of factors such as price, the financial strength of the provider, its investment performance, quality of customer service and the provider's administrative ability; and
- may be self-employed, part of an intermediary network or be employed by an organisation which has chosen to offer the products from all companies round the market place.

Both types of adviser have to be authorised and to be registered with the FSA. This authorisation usually involves passing specific qualifications (e.g. Certificate for Financial Advisers – CeFA) and remaining competent. For mortgage advice the

Mortgage Board has introduced training and competence requirements – in particular that registered firms must ensure that, by the end of 2002, all their advisers who provide an advice and recommendation service (i.e. service level (a) defined by the Code) have acquired an appropriate qualification. The acceptable qualifications are the Certificate in Mortgage Advice and Practice (CeMAP) or the Mortgage Advice Qualification (MAQ).

3.4 When dealing with advice to a customer, the concept of 'best advice' is paramount. Each organisation offering regulated financial services products must have its own code of conduct (which is in line with FSA regulations) to which it advisers adhere to. These codes of conduct will cover the following areas:

- *Confirming status – ensuring that an adviser has business cards which state the regulatory status of the firm involved. A terms of business letter should also be given to customers which sets out the adviser's status in more detail.*

- *Know your customer – so that the most appropriate advice can be given it is very important that the adviser understands as fully as possible the clients current financial position and their future aims and aspirations. Usually a detailed questionnaire is completed to establish this information.*

- *Best advice – as we have seen above, tied advisers give advice within the context of the products available from the company they represent, by ensuring that no other products in their range would better meet the clients' needs. When they cannot make a recommendation they have to say so.*
  Independent advisers must give best advice having assessed all the products available in the market recommending a suitable product and suitable company. The term 'best' is difficult to define precisely but all advisers must be able to show that they have taken reasonable steps to ensure the suitability of their recommendations.

- *Best execution – this should not be confused with 'best advice' and refers to trying to get the best possible terms for a customer in terms of price. It does not apply to 'packaged' products but would apply, for instance, to the commission charged in respect of share purchase.*

- *Suitability of products – having established the customer's needs, the product recommended must be suitable for those needs.*

- *Customers understanding of risk – if the product has an element of risk attached to the return this risk should be made clear to the customer. You may have seen the health warning 'the value of your investment may fall as well as rise' on product literature.*

- *Customer documentation – there are strict rules governing the type of documentation which must be retained and how long it should be kept for.*

- Strict rules also apply to customers' money in that it must be kept separate form the firm's money and kept in a separate deposit account. These money cannot be used to offset a firm's borrowings.

- Execution only – this is another term that you may find used. This term relates to situations where a customer decides to buy a product without having taken any advice. It is important for advisers to ensure that they have signed confirmation from the customer that they have bought the product on this basis to protect both parties.

3.5   The role of the introducer – introducers identify leads for onward referral to financial advisers. In this the role the introducer must not offer any advice and must not give the customer the impression that they are offering advice. They must be careful not to discuss in detail how a customer feels about an investment or its performance or plans they may have for the investment of money. Introducers shouldn't get drawn into discussion with the customer about their investment arrangements, financial objectives, risk profile or make any recommendations.

Introducers are able to gather factual information about the customer's existing arrangements.

The next sections looks at the various financial products that are available to customers. At the beginning of each section there is information about regulation of the product where you see a symbol like this:

Please read the 'health warning' so you understand the regulatory aspects as they apply to you.

4.0

Pensions

To some people retirement may seem a long way off. Before the existing state pension scheme was introduced there was no way of providing income for people in their old age other than what they managed to save themselves. Many people who were successful in business relied on the sale of their company to give them sufficient capital for their retirement. In the past, governments have provided a state pension. However, as we have seen from earlier sections, this cannot be fully relied upon to maintain an individual's standard of living into retirement.

Successive governments have offered tax benefits and other incentives to encourage people to save for adequate retirement pensions for themselves, rather than depending on the state retirement benefit and other social security benefits. Financial services organisations have been quick to enter this potentially very large market, where customers are attracted to tax efficient ways of saving for retirement.

There are various ways that pensions can be funded for people. This may depend on a person's type of employment and his age when starting a pension fund. There are a number of different schemes available including:

- *State pension schemes.*
- *Occupational pension schemes.*
- *Personal pension plans.*
- *Stakeholder pensions.*

We will look at each of these in turn. But first:

As pensions are a very important long-term investment, based on the stock market, this is a regulated product. Whilst it is important for you to understand how they work you must not give any advice or make recommendations to customers unless you are authorised to do so.

4.1   *State pension schemes* – the current state pension schemes are funded on a 'pay as you go' basis, which means that current National Insurance contributions from the working population are paid out as pension benefits to those entitled to receive them.

Pensions are payable from state retirement age, which is 65 for men and 60 for women. By the year 2020 the retirement age will have been equalised at 65 for everyone.

There are currently two state pension schemes:

- **The basic state pension** – *this is set at approximately 25% of the national average earnings level. The current pension (2001/2002) for a single person is £72.50 per week. A married couple (where the wife has not made her own National Insurance contributions) is £115.90 per week. Couples who have fully contributed can each receive the full single person's rate*
- **The state earnings-related pension (SERPS)** – *unlike the basic pension it is available only to employed persons who are paying 'Class 1' National Insurance contributions. Self-employed people cannot be members of SERPS. Employed people are obliged to be in SERPS unless they 'contract out' (elect to not be part of SERPS), or are contracted out by their employer on the basis of membership of*

the employer's pension scheme. Contracting out is permitted only if the employer, or the individual, provides an acceptable alternative pension provision. The element of National Insurance that would have gone into the SERPS scheme can be reclaimed from the government by a pension fund and added to this investment.

The objective of SERPS was originally to boost pension provision from 25% of national average earnings to 50% of national average earnings. Because of the ageing population it is thought that there is likely to be a scaling-down of prospective benefits (which are determined by a complex formula) and there is every likelihood of further reductions in the future.

4.2   *Occupational schemes* – employers often establish pension schemes for some or all of their employees. A good scheme is generally viewed by management as a means of attracting and retaining good quality staff. However, employers can no longer insist that membership of their scheme should be a condition of employment and employees can make their own arrangements if they wish.

Employers do not generally contribute to an individual's private pension arrangements whereas they often contribute substantial amounts to their own scheme. As a broad guide it is, therefore, generally recommended that most employees should join, or remain in their employers scheme if one is available.

Think

What are the pension arrangements with your employer?

Most occupational schemes, unlike the state schemes, are not run on a pay as you go basis. They are run on a 'funded' or 'advance' funded basis, which means that contributions are invested and built up into a fund from which it is expected that future pensions will be paid. There are two types of scheme:

- **Final salary schemes** – *these are schemes in which the pension benefits payable are based on a proportion of the final remuneration, the actual proportion being related to the length of an individual's membership of the pension scheme.*
- **Money purchase scheme** – *in this case there is no fixed pension benefit. Agreed contribution levels are paid by employers (and possibly employees) into a fund which is invested to produce lump-sums which will be available at employees' retirement dates. The level of pension received depends on:*
  - *the amounts contributed;*
  - *the success of the investment of the contributions; and*

    o   *the rate of return available when using the final lump-sum to purchase a pension annuity.*

There are a number of tax benefits associated with occupational schemes, including:

- *Tax relief on an employee's contribution at the highest rate of tax.*
- *Corporation tax relief on an employer's contribution.*
- *Exemption from capital gains tax on scheme investments.*
- *A tax free lump-sum which can generally be taken on retirement.*

The government imposes certain restriction on how much money can be put into and out of pension schemes because of these tax benefits.

It has been estimated that less than 1% of all occupational pension scheme members will obtain the maximum permitted benefits. There are various reasons for this, the most common being:

- *Their employer's scheme provides benefits that are less than the maximum allowed (e.g. where pensions are not based on full gross remuneration).*
- *Changes of employer have reduced their overall entitlement.*

Occupational scheme members whose prospective benefits are below the permitted maximum are entitled to make further personal contributions to an arrangement designed to make up this shortfall. Such contributions are known as **'Additional Voluntary Contributions' (AVCs)**. Since April 1988 it has been obligatory for company pension schemes to provide facilities for employees to pay AVCs into the scheme.

There are of course limitations on how much additional contribution an employee can make:

- *The contributions must not be such that they lead to the individual's overall pension benefits exceeding the maximum permitted levels.*
- *The individual's total contributions (AVCs plus employee contributions to the basic scheme) must not exceed 15% of their gross remuneration subject to an overall maximum of 15% of the earnings cap (£95,400 – 2001/2002).*

4.3   **Personal pension plans** – these are individual pension arrangements for people have relevant earnings from 'non-pensionable' employment. This includes self-employed sole traders, business partners, employees whose employers do not provide a pension scheme and employees who chose not to join their employers scheme.

Retirement benefits can be taken from a personal pension plan at any chosen age between 50 and 75. It is not necessary to actually retire in order to take the benefits. Special rules apply to certain occupations; for instance the Inland Revenues rules allow the benefits for professional sports people to be taken at much younger ages – in some cases as low as 35.

Personal pension plans are always 'money purchase' arrangements, which means that the amount of pension payable depends on the level of contributions paid, the investment performance of the fund and the pension annuity rates available on retirement. Most pension providers offer a wide choice of funds. The pension is not in any way directly related to the client's income at retirement, as it would be in a 'final salary' occupational scheme.

The main tax advantages associated with personal pensions are broadly in line with those for occupational schemes and other pension arrangements:

- *Contributions (within permitted limits) attract relief at the client's highest rate of tax.*
- *The invested funds are exempt from tax on capital gains (the amount the pension fund accumulates over time).*
- *Up to 25% of the accumulated fund can be taken as a tax-free lump-sum at the time when the pension payments commence. The remainder must be used to buy a pension annuity.*

Strict limits are imposed on the amount that can be contributed each year into a personal pension because of the beneficial tax treatment they attract. Maximum contribution rates are a set percentage of 'net relevant' earnings. This percentage depends on the age of the individual at the start of the tax year.

The contribution rates are as follows:

Age at 6 April	Contribution percentage of net relevant earnings
Up to age 35	17.5%
35–45	20.0%
46–50	25.0%
51–55	30.0%
56–60	35.0%
61–75	40.0%

There is an upper limit on the amount that can be contributed to a pension and for the tax year 2001–2002 the upper limit that could be contributed by someone in the oldest age range would be £38,160.

The authorities do, however, recognise that earnings levels – particularly for self-employed people – can vary from year-to-year. They are also aware that a self-employed person's accounts may not be finalised until some time after the period to which they relate. The rules about contribution levels have, therefore, been made flexible enough to enable people to make use, in the current tax year of unused contribution allowances from earlier years.

4.4   *Stakeholder pensions* – even before their election victory in 1997, the Labour party put forward their concept of a stakeholder pension. The stakeholder pension is a central part of Labour plans to reform welfare provision in the UK. Some of the reasons for this new idea were as follows:

- *There had been mis-selling of personal pensions.*
- *Four million people earning between £9,000 and £20,000 per year make no contribution to a pension at all.*
- *There was a need for a flexible and portable pension that could be transferred without penalty.*
- *The lack of trust of occupational pension schemes after the Maxwell affair.*
- *The need to provide better advice and education on retirement planning.*
- *The poor value offered by some private pension arrangements.*

Additionally, the new stakeholder pensions offered by financial service providers have the following features:

- *Lower charges – a maximum of 1% with no entry or exit charges (although after the introduction of the stakeholder pension a number of existing pension fund providers lowered their charging rates).*
- *Greater flexibility – relating to frequency and amount of contributions, individuals are also able to contract out of SERPS.*
- *A simplified tax regime – similar to the personal pension, however, higher rate tax must be claimed back via annual tax assessment.*

The biggest difference is that an individual does not have to be working or earning to contribute to a stakeholder pension. Non-earners can contribute and still reclaim tax-relief at the basic rate. They can contribute a maximum of £3,600 per year on this basis. The individual may pay in more than this if they are earning, to a maximum of the contribution limits for personal pensions based on age and income.

All schemes are based on a money purchase basis and the contributions invested to create a fund, which will be used to provide income for life when the individual retires.

Note

Who might benefit from saving in this way that hasn't previously been able to benefit from contributing to a pension scheme?

People who will benefit from this type of saving through a pension fund are:

- *Those on low incomes.*
- *Housewives or carers.*
- *People who are unable to work because of illness or disability.*
- *People who change roles frequently and perhaps have periods when they do not work.*

4.5   *Opportunities for lead generation:*

Note

What type of pension products do financial service providers offer to personal customers?

- *Personal Pensions.*
- *Stakeholder Pensions.*

Note

What might be the lifestyle changes where you might be able to spot an opportunity for a customer to be introduced to an adviser?

These opportunities might be:

- *Leaving university, starting work.*
- *Changing jobs, from company-to-company, from employed to self-employed.*
- *Moving house – it might be time to review their finances.*
- *Children leaving home – time to divert some spare cash into their retirement provision.*

Note

What banking transactions might alert you to a customer who could benefit from a pensions review with an adviser?

These transactions might be:

- *Change of address.*
- *Mortgage application.*
- *Loan application.*
- *Opening a saving account for long-term savings.*

5.0
Life assurance

Life assurance policies are products for which the payment of benefits depends upon circumstances related to the death or survival of a person or persons. In recent years, however, life assurance companies have broadened their scope to include policies related to sickness and accident cover. We will look at these in Section 6.

As life assurance is a very important long-term investment, based on the stock market, this is a regulated product. Whilst it is important for you to understand how it works you must not give any advice or make recommendations to customers unless you are authorised to do so.

5.1   *Historical background* – life assurance began in the UK as an adjunct to marine insurance, with the lives of sea-faring men being insured for a limited period, perhaps for the duration of the voyage or for one year. Initially the same premium rate was charged in each case whatever the age of the person being insured.

In the late 18th century, James Dodson developed a scientific basis on which people of any age could be offered life assurance at a more appropriate premium. Using data he had collected from gravestones from all over the UK, he produced a set of mortality tables (tables of death rates). Dodson was instrumental in establishing a life assurance company, which, by using the methods he had developed, offered cover on a fair and equitable basis. It become known as Equitable Life and the company still survives today.

From that time, scientific life assurance has been based on estimates of the future levels of three main factors that affect premiums to be charged and the subsequent profitability of the business. These are:

* *Mortality rates – these determine when and how claims will be paid out.*
* *Investment returns – the company can invest its funds to await the time when they will be paid out.*
* *Expenses – there are costs of running the business, including staff salaries, premises, marketing expenses and so on.*

5.2   *Modern life assurance products* – one type of savings contract offered by life assurance companies is endowment assurance policy. This policy pays out a specific sum (known as the 'sum assured') at the end of a specific term or upon the death of the life assured. These types of savings product are generally viewed as long-term savings. The policyholder's investment is made in the form of regular premiums to the company throughout the term of the policy. There a number of variations, the most common of which are:

- *With-profit endowment – this policy has a fixed basic sum assured and a fixed regular premium. In addition to the sum assured, the policyholder is entitled to share in the profits of the life assurance company. The company distributes its profits among policyholders by annually declaring bonuses that become part of the policy benefits and are payable at the same time and in the same circumstances to the sum assured. There are two types of bonus:*
  - *reversionary bonus – normally declared each year and once they have been allocated to a policy they cannot be removed by the company; and*
  - *terminal bonuses – a bonus is added to a with-profit policy when a death or maturity claim becomes payable. Unlike reversionary bonuses, it does not become part of the policy benefits until the moment of death or the maturity claim. This means that the company can change the terminal bonus rate or even remove the bonus altogether if it wishes to. These types of bonuses tend to reflect the level of investment gains, which the company has made over the term of the policy, so the rate of bonus often varies according to the length of time that the policy has been in force.*

Think

Consider this:

> If a number of life-assurance companies had recently reduced their terminal bonus rates, what might that indicate about the state of the stock market where their funds are invested?

A variation of the with-profit endowment policy is known as the low-cost endowment.

Advantages were seen to include:

- *A single large fund giving investors access to a wide spread of investments.*
- *The life company make all the investment decisions and policyholders need have no financial expertise at all.*
- *The policy has a minimum sum assured and investment performance is usually characterised by steady growth.*

The endowment policy has been used in the past for mortgage repayment purposes, however, recently, when policies matured, there were insufficient funds to repay the mortgages. Many mortgage lenders have decided not to promote this type of mortgage repayment vehicle.

- Unit-linked endowment – *the first unit-linked policies were introduced in the late 1950s and represented a revolutionary change in the way in which policies were designed. The development reflected the policyholders' desire to link investment returns more directly to the stock market, or even specific sectors of the market.*

  This is how the policy works – when a premium is paid, the amount of the premium – less any deductions for expenses – is applied to the purchase of 'units' in a chosen fund. A 'pool' of units gradually builds up and at the maturity date the policyholder receives an amount equal to the total value of all the units then allocated to the policy. Most unit-linked endowments also provide a fixed death benefit on death before the end of the term. The cost of providing this cover is taken from the policy each month by cashing in sufficient units from the 'pool'.

  Over the longer term, most successful unit-linked endowments have shown better returns than with-profit endowments. Unlike with-profit endowments, however, unit-linked policies do not provide any guaranteed minimum return at maturity.

  Advantages include:
  - *there is a wide range of funds to suit all investment requirements;*
  - *fund prices are readily available in the press, enabling policyholders to calculate how many units are allocated to their policy each time a premium is paid and how much their portfolio of units is worth; and*
  - *investment returns are directly related to the performance of the stock market or other underlying investments. This means the policyholder participates in any profits made by the fund manger but also any losses as well.*

- Unitised with-profit endowment – *these policies have been available since the late 1980s, when they were introduced in an attempt to combine the security of the with-profits policy with the greater potential for reward offered by the unit-linked approach. As with unit-linking, premiums are used to purchase units in a fund and the benefits paid out on a claim depend on the number of units allocated and the current price of units.*

  The difference lies in the fact that unit prices increase by the addition of bonuses which, like the reversionary bonuses on a with-profit policy, cannot be taken away once they have been added. This means that the unit price cannot fall and the value of the policy, if it is held until death or until the end of the specified term, is guaranteed.

  If the policy is surrendered (cashed in before its maturity date), however, a deduction is made from the value of the units. This deduction will depend upon the state of the market at the time of surrender and is known as a 'market value adjustment'.

5.3   *Opportunities for lead generation:*

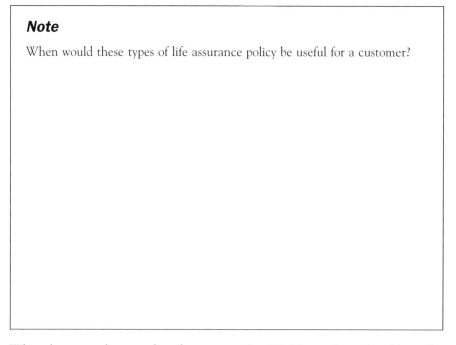

> **Note**
>
> When would these types of life assurance policy be useful for a customer?

When they wanted to save for a future event (say 10–20 years hence) and have the peace of mind to know that if anything were to happen to them, then there would be funds available to cover the event they were saving for. For example:

- *Parents or grandparents saving for children's university education, wedding, 21st birthday present.*
- *A couple who on retirement would like an additional lump sum in addition to that which their pensions were due to pay out.*

6.0
Personal protection insurance

Most people have some form of insurance to protect them against the financial effects of adversity. In some cases it is compulsory – for instance for car drivers on public roads. In may other cases it is wise to insure against loss of (or damage to) items that are too valuable to replace out of normal income, such as a house and its contents.

These examples relate to general insurance, which we will look at in section 9. Personal protection insurance relates to the adverse financial effects that can be caused by death or illness.

As personal protection insurance is a very important long-term investment, based on the stock market, this is a regulated product. Whilst it is important for you to understand how it works you must not give any advice or make recommendations to customers unless you are authorised to do so.

6.1 *'It won't happen to me'* – one of the main reasons that people fail to make provision for these adverse effects is that they believe 'it won't happen to me'. Sadly government statistics show that there is a greater chance than most people realise that it could.

Think

Consider these figures:

> The probability of dying before age 65 is about one in five for males in the UK.
>
> Over 150,000 males between 20 and 65 will die in the UK in a typical year.
>
> 600,000 males in the same age group will be off work for more than six months due to illness.
>
> Of those who have been off work due to illness for over 6 months, over 70% will have been off work for more than two years or more and well over 50% for three years or more.
>
> Every year more than 200,000 people in the UK are diagnosed as suffering from cancer, 100,000 have a stroke.
>
> Approximately one in six men aged between 45 and 65 will suffer a heart attack.
>
> Could these people say 'it won't happen to me'?

6.2 *What can personal protection insurance can be used for?* – there are a variety of uses:

- Family protection – *the death or long-term sickness of a breadwinner can leave a family with large debts and no income to support their standard of living. The situation may be just as severe on the death or illness of a dependent spouse, as this could leave the breadwinner with the choice between giving up work to look after the children or covering the expense of employing someone to look after them.*

- Debt protection – *when a mortgage or other loan is being repaid largely from the income of one individual, the death of that individual can result in failure to make the repayments, possibly leading to the loss of any property used as security for the loan.*

- Tax mitigation – *when an individual leaves a substantial 'estate' (the deceased's assets) to someone else when they die, the recipients may find that they have to pay inheritance tax out of the value of the estate. If they cannot, or do not wish to dispose of the assets, a suitable 'life' policy could be used. The only exception to this need is if the estate is left to the deceased's spouse.*

- Business protection – *the death of an important employee (known as 'key' employee) could have a devastating effect on the profits of a company. Protection against the financial consequences of losing such an employee should be part of a company's planning.*

    Another example, is where in a business partnership one of the partners die and the remainder wish to buy out this partner's share without having to realise the assets of the business to do so. In many partnerships, such as firms of solicitors and accountants, much of the value of the business is made up of that intangible asset of 'goodwill'. This takes into account the reputation of the business as a whole. This means that selling the business as a whole would be something the partners would wish to avoid at all costs. Life assurance on each of the partners' lives can provide a solution.

6.3 The type of personal protection insurance that covers the adverse financial affects of death falls into two main categories:

- Whole of life assurance – *the sum assured is payable on the death of the life assured whenever that death occurs. The policy has no fixed time limit and remains in force – provided that premiums continue to be paid. The policy is brought to its end by the payment of a death claim or until it is surrendered (cashed in) by the policyholder for a reduced sum.*

    Premiums may be payable throughout the lifetime of the policy or they may be limited to a particular term or to some fixed age, such as 60 or 65. These policies can be issues in a number of different formats as described in section 6.

The unit-linked format is particularly useful for whole life assurance because it provides the flexibility to change the level of cover on a policy as the individual's financial situation changes. Since the cost of the cover is taken monthly by cashing in an appropriate number of the policy's fund of units, changing the level of cover can be achieved by increasing or decreasing the number of units cashed.

Some unit-linked whole or life policies include additional benefits, such as total and permanent disability benefit and waiver of premium in the event of sickness. Such policies are often referred to as universal whole of life contracts.

- Term assurance – In this case the sum assured is payable only if the life assured dies before the end of the specified term. If the life assured survives the term, the cover ceases and no payment or refund of premiums is made. Similarly, if the policy is cancelled part way through the term, it has no cash surrender value. The term can be from one month to 30 years or more, although if a very long term is required, it may be better to consider a whole of life assurance.

A number of different varieties of term assurance have been developed to satisfy a range of needs:

  o Level term assurance – the sum assured remains level throughout the term. This can be used for a loan where the customer is covering interest only and the capital amount is not reducing.

  o Decreasing term assurance – the sum assured reduces over the term of the policy, but the premiums remain the same. The sum assured may reduce in equal annual amounts or in some other specified manner. The most common application of this type of policy is to cover a loan or mortgage where the capital is being repaid over the term of the mortgage.

  o Family income benefits – this policy is different in that the sum assured is payable not as a lump sum but as a series of regular monthly or quarterly instalments from the date of death until the end of the policy term.

  o Convertible term assurance – this is a term assurance (normally level term) that includes an option to convert the policy into a whole of life or endowment policy of the same sum assured without further evidence of health. The cost of the option is usually an additional 10%–15% of the premium.

  o Renewable/increasable term assurance – this term assurance includes an option, which can be exercised at the end of the term, to renew the policy for an additional term and to increase the sum assured by a specified amount, again without further evidence of health.

  o Pension term assurance – people who are eligible to take out a personal pension plan are also permitted to take out a term assurance policy either separately or in conjunction with their pension plan. The main advantage of doing this is that the premiums paid on the term assurance attract tax relief where as conventional term assurance premiums do not.

6.4   *Permanent Health Insurance (PHI)* is designed to replace income in the event of an individual being able to work due to illness, disability or accident.

The term of PHI cannot be extended beyond a person's intended (or actual) retirement date. There is a maximum permitted benefit level which most companies set at around 60–65% of earnings, less the basic state incapacity level. The maximum benefit rule is enforced by the companies to prevent excessive claims that would no doubt ensue if policyholders could receive more income when sick than they would if they returned to work.

Each PHI policy is subject to a 'deferred' period, which is the time that must elapse after the policyholder falls ill before benefit payments can commence. The minimum deferred period is four weeks or the policyholder can chose 13 weeks, 26 weeks one year or even two years. The longer they take before the benefit starts generally the cheaper the premiums become.

When payments commence they are paid, free of tax, until the claimant recovers, reaches retirement age or dies. The word 'permanent' in the policy title refers to the fact that – provided premiums are paid – the insurer cannot cancel the policy simply on the grounds of heavy claims experience.

Premiums vary according to the age, gender and occupation of the policyholder as well as on the policy term and benefit. People whose jobs are more dangerous, physically demanding or more stressful generally pay higher premiums.

6.5   *Critical Illness cover* – although benefit payments from this type of policy relate to sickness rather than death, they are very different from permanent health insurance policies. In particular:

- *The benefit is payable on the diagnosis of one of a specified range of illnesses and conditions. It is not necessary for the claimant to be off work and the benefit is paid irrespective of whether the claimant subsequently recovers.*
- *The benefit is in the form of a tax-free lump-sum, not in regular income. Once the benefit has been paid, the policy ceases and the sum assured could not be paid again, even if the policyholder subsequently suffered another of the specified illnesses.*

Each company has its own list of illnesses covered but they normally include:

- *Most forms of cancer.*
- *Heart attack.*
- *Stroke.*
- *Coronary heart disease requiring surgery.*
- *Major organ transplants.*
- *Multiple sclerosis.*
- *Total and permanent disability.*

The cover from some policies also includes payment of the sum assured on death if it occurs before a claim has been paid for diagnosis of a specific disease.

6.6   *Opportunities for lead generation:*

Note

Who would benefit from taking out personal protection insurance?

- *Families who want to protect against death or illness of a breadwinner.*
- *People who have few of their own resources to fall back on if they are ill.*
- *People who are taking out a large loan or mortgage.*
- *People who are making a will who have assets over the inheritance tax threshold.*
- *People whose employers give little or no sickness cover.*
- *People who are worried about the levels of care provided by the National Health Service.*

7.0

Investments

In Unit 1, section 7, we considered customer needs and how people accumulate wealth. We are now going to look at some other ways that people may chose to invest that wealth through financial products and services that are not related to life assurance products. To recap we said that people can accumulate wealth by regular saving or by acquiring a lump-sum. They can then invest these money in a variety of ways. People will be sensitive to the level of risk they take and the degree of accessibility they have to their funds. This will be different for everyone and the role of an authorised financial advisor is to establish what these sensitivities are.

Added to this will be the individual's tax position, which will be discussed later in this section. The government has in recent years tried to encourage the population to save by offering tax-free investment opportunities:

- *Some National Savings Products.*
- *Personal Equity Plans – PEPs (no new plans are available).*
- *Tax exempt special savings accounts – TESSAs (no new accounts available).*
- *Individual savings accounts – ISAs.*

Investments have the potential to produce either income or capital growth (where the underlying value increases over time) or a proportion of either. We will now take a closer look at some of the main investment 'vehicles'.

7.1 *Savings accounts* – these will be in the form of the range of offerings that most retail financial services organisations provide.

The main attraction for savers is that they consider their money to be secure. This is certainly true in terms of the stability of the financial services provider as an organisation. Reputable financial services providers will belong to the Financial Services Compensation Scheme, which provides additional protection to depositors and investors in the event of the collapse of a financial services provider. Further details are in Unit 4, Section 3.

It is also true that this type of saving is risk free – if a saver deposits £100 in their account they will be able to withdraw £100 the following month or year. However, as we have seen in previously (Unit 1, section 2), in times of high inflation the real value of the deposit is being eroded.

Whilst this saving is secure, the rates of interest it earns do fluctuate. Again if the rate of interest the money is earning is less than the annual rate of inflation the value of the investment will be eroded in real terms. Savings accounts are useful for putting money aside that will be used in the short-term or for customers that are particularly risk averse.

Note

What sort of savings or deposit accounts does your organisation provide?

How are these different?

Many accounts have 'tiered' interest rates – the rate of interest increases with higher balances. Other features include different 'periods of notice' – money can be tied up for usually seven days, one month or three months, where notice is required to be given before the money can be withdrawn. If funds are withdrawn without notice being given there is usually a penalty to be paid. Another way of rewarding savers, who leave their funds in their account, is to give interest bonuses. Another way is to pay interest more frequently.

Think

Consider this:

> Why is an account that pays interest quarterly more advantageous than an account where interest is paid annually?

The account that pays interest quarterly is more advantageous because the saver can earn interest on the interest they have received. When savers are comparing accounts they need to look at this as part of their decision about which one to chose.

The rates quoted by many financial services organisations will give the gross rate per annum as a percentage, which is the rate applicable before deducting any tax. They will also give the 'Annual Equivalent Rate' or the 'AER' as a percentage. This is a notional (estimated) rate that shows the gross interest rate as if paid including all the interest that would be paid in the year. The following table shows an example of the difference:

	Gross rate per annum	AER
Monthly interest account	3.68%	3.75%
Annual interest account	3.68%	3.68%

All interest (except that paid to non-residents) is paid net of basic rate tax.

7.2 *Individual savings accounts (ISAs)* replaced PEPs and TESSAs from 6th April 1999 as the main tax-free savings schemes. Existing PEP holdings have not been affected and existing TESSAs will be able to run to maturity. PEPs were a way of allowing people to hold shares in a tax efficient form up to an annual limit and TESSAs were a way for people to hold cash in a tax efficient form, again up to certain annual limits.

The Labour government's purpose in introducing ISAs was to develop the savings habit among the less well-off and to ensure that tax-relief on savings is fairly distributed. Whether these aims will be achieved remains open to considerable doubt because the complex nature of the product seems unlikely to appeal to the less financially sophisticated. ISAs have been a new way for individuals to save towards mortgage repayment of interest-only mortgages (see section 8).

Any ISA based on the stock market is deemed an investment is, therefore, a regulated product. Whilst it is important for you to understand how it works you must not give any advice or make recommendations to customers unless you are authorised to do so.

There are three possible components of ISAs:

- *Stocks and shares – those shares of companies, wherever they are incorporated and officially listed on a recognised stock exchange, and government stock from any country in the EU, can be held directly in an ISA. This does not include shares already held by the investor. However shares received from an approved savings related share option scheme (SAYE) or company profit sharing scheme can be transferred in:*
  - *Cash, including taxable National Savings accounts and bank and building society accounts.*
  - *Single-premium life assurance policies.*

Each year savers have the option of either taking an ISA with a single manager who offers an account that can accept the full subscription (a Maxi ISA) or to go to separate managers for each of the two or more components (Mini ISAs).

For a Maxi ISA the limits are as follows (until 2006):

- *£7,000 in total, of which no more than £3,000 can be cash and £1,000 a single-premium life policy. If the investor wishes to use shares, they can do for the full amount.*

For Mini ISAs the limits are as follows (until 2006):

- *£3,000 into a cash ISA.*
- *£1,000 into a single premium policy.*
- *£3,000 into a stocks and shares ISA.*

It can be seen that if the investor wishes to invest solely in shares, then the Maxi ISA would be their choice. Also note here that unauthorised staff may talk to customers about cash ISAs.

There is no minimum period that the ISA must be held for and withdrawals can be made at any time without jeopardising the tax-free element. This is different to the TESSA that had both time limits and tax payable on interest withdrawals before the end of the investment period.

The government has introduced a set of standards – Cost Access and Terms (CAT) standards – intended to help less knowledgeable investors choose a suitable deal. ISAs that meet these standards will be 'CAT' marked. The government has stressed that the CAT mark is not a seal of approval and it may well be that many ISAs, particularly those investing in the stocks and shares component, will be marketed without being CAT marked. This is because cost restrictions are so tight that they may preclude schemes that allow the cost of giving advice to potential investors.

7.3   *Shares* – It was a stated aim of the Conservative governments of 1980s that Britain should become a 'share-owning democracy' to a greater extent than it had before. Although it is true that the public has on the whole become more aware of the nature of investment in shares, any increase in share related investment by individuals has been mainly through indirect channels such as unit trusts (see Unit 3, section 3.4) than the direct purchase of company shares.

Any shares or products based on shares (e.g. unit trusts) are a regulated product. Whilst it is important for you to understand how they work you must not give any advice or make recommendations to customers unless you are authorised to do so.

Direct investment in shares remains, for the most part, the territory of the large institutions such as pension funds, unit trusts and life assurance companies who hold over 70% of the shares issued in the UK. The main exception to this was in the privatisation issues (such as British Telecom), which, perhaps due to their novelty value, did catch the attention of the investing public. Shares can be bought for their capital growth or for their income potential through dividends.

The most common form of shares are ordinary shares, also known as equities because they represent a direct investment in the equity of a company. This means that holders of ordinary shares are in effect part owners of a company. Ordinary shares normally confer the following rights:

* *To participate in the distribution of the company's profits in the form of dividends.*
* *To contribute to decisions about how the company is run, by voting at shareholders' meetings and electing a board of directors.*

Shares are traded on the Stock Exchange and the price at which they change hands depends on various factors including:

- *The current and expected future profitability of the company.*
- *The quality and track record of the management.*
- *The economic prospects of the industry in which it operates and of other related industries.*
- *The state of the national and international economy.*

In assessing the suitability of shares, investors may take into account the following factors:

- Earnings per share – *this is equal to the company's profit after tax (net profit) divided by the number of shares it has issued. This gives an indication of profitability, but it is not the amount of dividend to which a shareholder is entitled on each of their shares. This is because a company may choose not to distribute all of its profits; some may be retained in the business, to finance expansion, for instance.*

This leads to the concept of:

- Dividend cover – *this is a factor that indicates how much of a company's profits were paid as dividends in a particular distribution (sharing of profit among shareholders). If, for example, 50% of profits is paid in dividends, the dividend is said to be covered twice, i.e. a dividend is paid once and could be paid once again. If 25% of profits are paid out as dividend then dividend is said to be covered four times, and so on. Cover of 2.0 or more is generally considered to be acceptable by investors, whereas a figure of 1.0 indicates that all the profit is being paid out as dividend (and, therefore, none retained and reinvested in the company). A figure of below one indicates that dividend is being paid out of retained surpluses from previous years.*
- Price/earnings ratio (P/E ratio) – *as its name suggests the P/E ratio is calculated as the share price divided by the earnings per share. It is generally considered to be a useful guide to a share's growth prospects. A ratio of 20 or more, for example, indicates that a share is doing well and can be expected to increase in value in the future. Such a share is likely to be relatively more expensive than others within the same market sector. A low ratio, less than about four, indicates that the market feels that the share has poor prospects of growth.*

When assessing P/E ratios it is important to compare them with those of companies within the same sector. For example, in the latter part of 1998 Marks and Spencer's share price and P/E ratio fell back sharply as investors were concerned about future profitability, given the uncertain economic climate and the company's poor sales performance compared to its competitors.

7.4 *Unit trusts* – as seen above, unit trusts are a very popular way for the private investor to invest on the stock exchange and achieve capital growth over a long-term period. A unit trust is a lump sum or regular savings investment created under a 'trust deed', a binding legal agreement. The deed is entered into between the promoters of the trust, known as the managers and the trustees. Both managers and trustees undertake certain obligations under the trust deed.

The trust is divided into units whereby each unit represents a fraction of the all the trust's assets. The managers are obliged under the trust deed to buy back units from any unit holders who wish to sell them.

As with certain other investments the price of units whenever the investor is selling is always lower than when the investor is buying. The price investors pay for units is known as the 'offer' price. The selling price when investors sell their units back to the trust manager is known as the 'bid' price. These two terms are often confused. There is a third price called the 'cancellation' price or the minimum bid price. The difference between the offer price and the cancellation price takes into account the full costs of buying and selling the underlying shares. However, because funds often have both buyers and sellers it is not always necessary to use this minimum price.

In exchange for spreading the risk across different shares through the purchase of units, investors pay initial setting up charges and an annual management fee.

7.5 *Taxation*: when considering any form of financial advice for investments the customer's tax position is very important. This is because, usually, customers wish to pay as little tax as possible and therefore want to make sure they can structure their investments in a tax efficient way.

We have already seen how the government set taxes via the budget in Unit 1. The following table shows the income tax reliefs (limits on amounts under which no tax is paid) and tax rates for the tax year 2001–2002.

Income tax rates

10% of first	£1,880
22% (20% for savings income) on next	£27,520
40% on income over	£29,400
Dividend income for basic rate tax payers	10.0%
Dividend income for higher rate tax payers	32.5%

Main Income tax reliefs

Personal allowance – basic	£4,535
Personal allowance – 65–74	£5,990
Personal allowance – 75 & over	£6,260
Children's tax credit at 10% *	£5,200

* This allowance is to parents with children under 16 and is bound by income criteria. It is reduced by £2 for each £3 of a claimant's income taxed at the higher tax rate

There are also special income tax reliefs and rates for married couples, where one of the partners was born before 6 April 1935.

A customer's personal allowance can be adjusted by the Inland Revenue to take into account taxable benefits that they may receive from their employers. These benefits can be in the form of company cars, medical health insurance and cheap loans. Their allowance may also be adjusted for under payments of tax in the previous year. Once these adjustments are done this gives the 'tax code' on which employers base their calculations for payment of tax to the Inland Revenue.

One of the reasons why a customer may invest on the stock market either directly or indirectly will be to attain capital growth. There are also limitations of this for individuals of:

Capital gains tax for individuals: *the first £7,500 of net gain is tax free, and then any gain over this amount will be taxed in the same way as for savings. The calculation of capital gains tax can be complex, as certain costs and allowances are taken into account.*

Inheritance tax: *the first £242,000 of a deceased estate (that is eligible for this tax) is tax-free. Any inheritance assets over this figure will attract a tax of 40%. There are also restrictions on what can be given as gifts, with reductions in the tax paid on a sliding slide for gifts given within seven years of death.*

7.6   *Opportunities for lead generation*

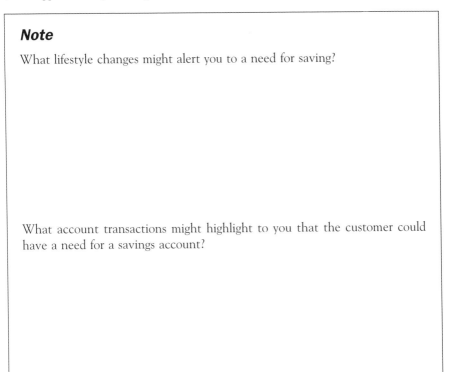

Note

What lifestyle changes might alert you to a need for saving?

What account transactions might highlight to you that the customer could have a need for a savings account?

Lifestyle changes could be:

- *A new job, that is better paid.*
- *Children leaving home.*
- *Moving to a smaller property that is cheaper to run.*

Account transactions could be:

- *Regular high balances – may have surplus funds.*
- *Just finished paying loan account – may be able to save the amount that was going to pay off the loan account.*
- *A large credit to the account – could be a lottery win, inheritance money or a loan from another provider!*

8.0
Mortgages

Mortgages are the most popular way of purchasing residential property in the UK. Historically, building societies were the main providers, but since deregulation of the financial markets in the 1980s, banks and specialist mortgage finance companies (Unit 1, section 6.6) have also offered mortgage and related products.

Some products associated with mortgages are regulated. Whilst it is important for you to understand how they work, you must not give any advice or make recommendations to customers unless you are authorised to do so.

8.1 Mortgages are long term loans, usually for 20 to 25 years made to people over the age of 18 and over (i.e. they are not minors and can legally borrow money). The amount of the loan can be anything up to 100% of the property value, though it is more usual to lend to a lower percentage. This is a result of the 'negative equity' problems experienced during the property slump of the 1990s when many house-holders found the value of their property was less than the amount they had borrowed to buy it. This can become a problem for the customer if they are unable to make repayments on their mortgage or should they wish to move house.

8.2 Most mortgages are made by legal charge. The borrower owns and lives in the property once the loan is made and the house purchased. The lender, however, takes a 'legal charge' over the deeds of the property giving them certain rights. In Scotland this is known as a 'standard security'.

The borrower, who mortgages the property for the duration of the loan, is known as the *mortgagor*. The lender, who has this interest in the property for the duration of the loan, is known as the *mortgagee*.

As we have said above, the mortgagee is given certain rights over the property and will normally insist that the borrower insures and maintains the property in an acceptable condition. In particular, if the borrower defaults on mortgage payments, the lender is entitled to take possession of the property and to sell it to recover the money owed. That step is, however, normally taken only as a last resort. Under the terms of a statement of practice established by the Mortgage Board problems of arrears – which generally arise from unforeseen circumstances such as redundancy or family breakdown – should be treated sympathetically and positively.

8.3 At the same time borrowers retain certain rights, in particular:
* *They have the right to repay the loan at any time (although this may be subject to*

an early repayment penalty if the borrower has chosen a 'fixed rate' or 'capped rate' mortgage).

- *Borrowers whose properties have been taken into possession by a lender are still entitled to repay the loan right up until the time when the property is sold.*
- *Borrowers are entitled to the remainder of the sale price after a loan has been repaid, so if the lender sells the property to repay the loan, any surplus must be paid over to the borrower.*

8.4   There are a number of financial elements of a mortgage transaction that of concern to a borrower. These are:

- *How much they can borrow.*
- *Interest rates.*
- *Length of term of the mortgage (usually linked to a person's intended retirement date).*
- *Monthly repayment figure.*
- *Method by which the loan is repaid.*

Think

Consider this:

> When an advisor is preparing a mortgage quote, if the length of the term of the mortgage is extended (and all the other factors remain the same) what will be the effect on the monthly repayment?
>
> What will be the effect on the overall amount repaid?

There will be quite a lot for the customer to think about when they ask for a quote and this is why most financial services organisations will have specialists who will undertake the mortgage adviser role. In the example above, the effect is that the monthly repayments will become less if the term of the mortgage is extended, however, the overall amount to be repaid will be more.

8.5   *Repayment methods* – there are two different ways of repaying a mortgage loan. These are the 'repayment' (or capital and interest) mortgage and the 'interest-only' mortgage. There is much debate over which is the better option for borrowers and in fact the costs are not dissimilar. Each type has its advantages and dis-advantages and indeed most lenders will allow customers to take their mortgage splitting the borrowing across both methods if appropriate.

- Repayment mortgages – *The borrower makes monthly payments to the lender consisting partly of interest and partly of capital repayment. The amount of capital outstanding, therefore, reduces over the period of the loan until it is fully repaid at the end of the term.*

  The relative proportions of capital and interest in the payment amount vary throughout the term as you can see from Figure 2.2. The outstanding capital amount reduces slowly in the early years of the loan but more quickly as time passes.

  In the unfortunate event of the borrower dying before the end of the mortgage term, the surviving family may have difficulty maintaining the payments and at worst may have to sell the property. Happily, separate life assurance can be taken out to cover this eventuality – a decreasing term assurance policy (see section 6.3). This type of policy is also known as mortgage protection assurance.

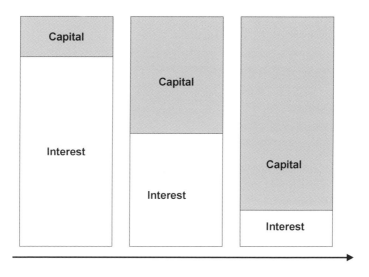

Time

Figure 2.2 *Capital and interest proportions over a 25-year period.*

- Interest only mortgages – *the monthly payments to the lender are made up solely of interest on the loan. No capital repayments are made to the lender during the term of the loan and the capital amount outstanding does not reduce at all. The monthly interest amount only changes if the mortgage interest rate increases or decreases. Figure 2.3 illustrates this.*

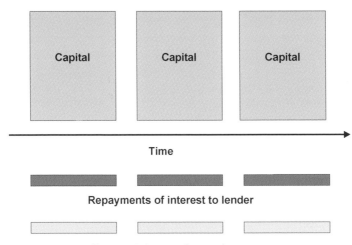

Figure 2.3 *Interest only mortgage.*

The borrower still has the responsibility of repaying the capital amount at the end of the term. This is usually achieved through the borrower making regular payments to an appropriate savings scheme, which should increase over time. It may well be that the lender will want to have sight of the savings scheme documentation to ensure that there will be sufficient capital in the scheme at its end. They may also want to hold the documents which relate to ownership of the scheme.

Note

From the savings schemes mentioned in section 6.0 Life policies and 8.0 Investments, which would be suitable for using for mortgage repayment?

The main savings schemes used for mortgage repayment are as follows:

- ISAs – *although extra life cover may be required.*
- Pensions – *again depending on the pension policy life cover may not be built in.*
- Unitised-linked endowments – *these would have to be checked on a regular basis usually after the first ten years to ensure the plan was growing at a sufficient rate.*
- Personal Equity Plans – *although new PEPs are no longer available customers may use existing plans.*
- Endowment assurances – *these are no longer as popular as they once were and many financial services organisations will no longer accept them as sufficient means of repaying an interest only mortgage.*

8.6 Mortgage options and interest rates

There are a number of different ways of repaying interest to suit different types of customer:

- Standard variable rate – *here the interest rate (and therefore the monthly repayment) will go up and down, without limit, in line with variations in the Bank of England's base rate. The main disadvantage with this method is that borrowers cannot easily predict future levels of repayment, which can cause budgeting problems.*
- Fixed rate – *the borrower is able to 'lock into' a fixed interest payment for a specified period, usually between one and five years. At the end of that period, the rate reverts to the lenders prevailing variable rate.*

  This scheme is popular with first-time buyers and others who want to be able to budget precisely. There is often an arrangement fee and there may be restrictions or penalties for early repayment or moving to another lender.
- Capped rate – *the interest rate has an upper fixed limit, known as a 'cap'. The lender's normal variable rate will apply, but it will be subject to a capped rate. Should the variable rate exceed the cap, the borrower has the advantage of paying the capped rate only. This is particularly useful when interest rates are likely to fall. There is normally a fee for this and a set period of time during which repayments are to be made.*
- Cap and collar rate – *this type of interest rate as a fixed upper rate (cap) and a fixed lower rate (collar). Again, this will be for set period of time, after which the variable rate will apply and there is normally a fee for this. This arrangement may suit borrowers who believe that interest rates are likely to rise.*
- Low start rate – *in the early years of this type of mortgage, some of the interest is not paid but is added to the outstanding capital. This may be appropriate for borrowers who expect their income to increase, but borrowers should beware of using it at times when house prices are likely to fall because it brings an increased danger of a negative equity situation.*

- Discounted rate – *this refers to a genuine discount off the normal variable rate, e.g. 2% discount for 12 months. After this the interest rate reverts to the standard variable rate. There are generally restrictions or penalties for redeeming the mortgage within a specified period, which may extend beyond the discount period. In the highly competitive mortgage market of recent years, offers of discounted mortgages have been used to attract first-time buyers and to tempt borrowers from other lenders.*
- Flexible mortgages – *there are various different types of this mortgage available and as they suggest they give the borrower a greater degree of flexibility than the other types of mortgages described above.*

  The most important feature of flexible mortgages is that the borrower is allowed to vary their mortgage payments. This means the borrower may overpay and underpay depending on the circumstances (within certain guidelines). Other features may include:
  - *the facility to borrow more money, within agreed limits for lump sum expenditure such as home improvements;*
  - *current account with cheque book and agreed overdraft facility;*
  - *credit card with an agreed spending limit;*
  - *debit cards; and*
  - *the interest rate option can be from any of the above rate options.*

Note

The flexible mortgage is a very popular type of mortgage attracting well over 10% of new mortgage lending.

Does your organisation promote this type of product?

If so, collect some information about it and familiarise yourself with it.

If not, look for a competitor who does offer it and see what the benefits are.

- Cashbacks – *as an alternative to discount off the variable rate, lenders may offer a cash sum once the mortgage has been completed (and money have been taken by the borrower). This sum usually varies according to the size of the mortgage loan. The terms of the cashback will provide for repayment of a proportion of the sum if the loan is redeemed within a specified number of years. Other incentives include offering to pay the customers' legal fees or free property survey/valuation fees.*

8.7   *Finding packages to suit customer* – when customers are thinking about looking for the right mortgage they will have a number of questions they will need to consider:

- *Can we afford this house?*
- *Can we afford the monthly repayments?*
- *How we got enough money for the deposit, the solicitor's fees, the estate agents fees, the removal men and so forth. It's easy to forget all these extras.*
- *Do we want to know that our monthly outgoings are going to be the same over the beginning of the mortgage?*
- *What do with think is going to happen with interest rates?*
- *How long would we want to fix our monthly repayments for?*
- *Are we likely to want to make any lump sum reductions to the mortgage at some time in the future?*

These questions link into the question of 'affordability' and it is part of the responsible lender's role to ensure that the customers can afford the house and are not getting carried away. Part of the role of the adviser is to find out the answers to these questions in discussion with the customer and then advise the customer on the right types of mortgage to suit their needs.

8.8   *Process of house purchase* – the whole process of buying a house can be very lengthy and stressful – as anyone who has been through the experience will say. The customer is relying on a good team of people to help them; from the mortgage lender, estate agent, solicitor, removal men, even down to the utilities who have to be contacted to be advised of the new owners. If you have been involved in house purchase, whether from a personal or professional perspective, then you will know that understanding what happens, and when, is useful when trying to make the deadlines agreed to. Set out in Figures 2.4a, 2.4b and 2.c is a simplified 'first-time buyer' scenario. It obviously becomes more complex if there is also a house to sell. It will be easier for customer contact staff within the financial services organisation to empathise with customers if they can understand what is involved during the house buying process.

Initially it is important that the customer provides all the necessary information when they complete their application form. Late receipt of this information can hold up their application and cause frustration. Such information will be such as;

last three months bank statements, last three wages slips, evidence of bonuses, identification, National Insurance numbers and so on.

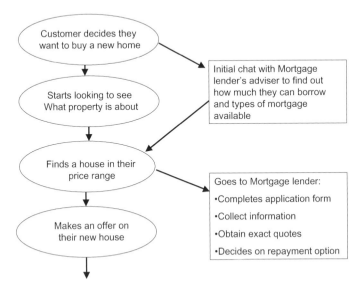

Figure 2.4a *Events to 'offer'.*

Before 'exchange' of contracts the customer is not legally bound and they can retract an offer if they wish. The seller is also not bound to stand by their acceptance of the offer and can accept a better one if they chose to. However, reputable estate agents will discourage this sort of behaviour if they can.

Figure 2.4b shows the events up to exchange. It is important that the valuation is appropriate for the mortgage taken. Some customers have a shock when the valuer reports defects that they weren't expecting or the market valuation is lower than the price they wanted to offer. This can be the point at which buyers decide to back out. For properties that are very old, Mortgage lenders recommend that customers have a 'full structural' survey, which is done by a qualified surveyor and will highlight any deficiencies that the building may have.

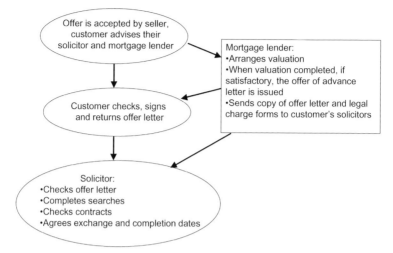

Figure 2.4b *Events up to 'Exchange'.*

The next diagram (Figure 2.4c) shows 'exchange' and 'completion'. Exchange refers to the signing and swapping of contracts between the two parties. Once this point is passed the buyer is legally obliged to purchase the property. If for some reason they wished to back out they would lose their deposit (usually 10% of the

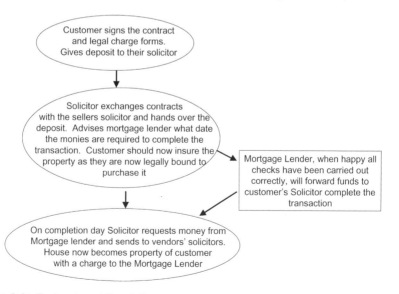

Figure 2.4c *Exchange and Completion.*

purchase price) and be liable for compensation to the seller. This is situation is highly unusual. As the buyer is now legally obliged to purchase the property, mortgage lenders and solicitors usually advise the purchaser to insure the property just in case anything were to happen to it before they move in.

Once all the legal checks have been completed they the parties will be ready to complete.

On completion day, once the money have been received by the seller's solicitors, the estate agent hands over the keys to the new buyer and they can move in.

It all sounds very straightforward, however, there are a multitude of things that can go wrong or hold things up. The whole process usually takes about six to eight weeks, however, sometimes this can be achieved more quickly.

9.0
General insurance

As will be seen in Unit 4, the Financial Services Authority is able to exercise investigations under the Financial Services Act 1987, the Banking Act 1987 and the Insurance Companies Act 1982. This means that if an organisation is conducting insurance business without the required authorisation or exemption, or is guilty of misconduct then the Financial Services Authority has the powers to deal with this organisation. The products themselves are not 'regulated', however, the general insurance industry has codes of conduct and good practice overseen by the General Insurance Standards Council (GISC). The GISC is able to carry out assessments that will confirm to the customer that the insurer is reputable and has employees that meet the required levels of competence.

General insurance cover for personal customers includes loss from:

- *Accident.*
- *Sickness.*
- *Fire and natural causes.*
- *Damage to property.*
- *Motor vehicle liability.*
- *Miscellaneous financial loss.*
- *Legal expenses.*

The types of protector policy will therefore relate to:

- *Cars and motorcycles.*
- *Travel.*
- *Personal injury.*
- *Home and contents.*

- *Pets.*
- *Caravans and boats.*
- *Legal expenses.*
- *Extended warranty on electrical goods.*

Most policies will cover anything where there will be a loss of or damage to property, liability to a third party or personal injury.

Insurance is offered to the 'market' by insurance companies or mutual companies and this can include the mainstream financial services organisations. These policies can also be offered by 'intermediaries', who act as a broker between the seller and the buyer of insurance. Their role has changed much over the recent years in the personal market and many people now buy directly from the provider, however, this has not been the case for commercial insurance, which is more complex.

9.1 *Nature of risk* – as with life assurance policies, risk is the inability to predict future events. All sorts of mishaps can happen to people and property and all these risks have some common factors:

- *Will the event take place at all?*
- *When will the event take place?*
- *Will there be a loss when an event happens?*

We all have our own views on risk and not everyone decides to insure against it, unless where it is compulsory such as car insurance. For example, only 35% of people insure the contents of their home and this will be because some people are more concerned about the risks that life presents.

Individuals will consider and evaluate the risks in a number of ways:

- *The level of* uncertainty *– how likely the event is to happen and sometimes we cannot predict what the future has in store.*
- *The level of* risk *– in terms of:*
  - *frequency of occurrence;*
  - *severity of the effects; and*
  - *cause of the loss and ways this can be reduced.*

Part of the role of the customer (also known as the proposer) who requires the insurance, is to supply the insurers with relevant information about the risk they would like to be insured against. This is usually collected on a 'proposal' form. It is the responsibility of the proposer to disclose all the material facts. This will include:

- *Name and address.*
- *Occupation.*
- *Personal details, including age – which is especially important for motor insurance – and health, if relevant.*

- *Subject matter of the insurance.*
- *Insurance history and claims record.*
- *The cover required.*
- *Risk-specific information – these are details relating to the item to be insured, e.g. does the property have a thatched roof or is it in an area liable to subsidence? Does the person partake of dangerous pastimes?*

9.2 *Assessing the risk* – once all the information has been collected it is passed to the underwriter. It is the underwriter's role to assess the level of risk presented by the proposer and the subject matter of the insurance.

During this process, the underwriter will make decisions about accepting the risk and, if so, should any special conditions should apply and what premium should be charged. It is this process of acceptance that gave rise to the name of 'underwriter', because when marine insurance first started the person accepting the risk would sign under the details of the risk to be insured.

Effectively, the greater the risk the higher the premium is likely to be. In the 'direct' motor insurance market, proposals that do not fall within strict underwriting parameters are usually rejected. This means that the costs of maintaining a highly skilled underwriting department are removed from the calculation of the premiums. Also, by only accepting restricted similar risks the calculation of premiums can become accurate and therefore more competitive.

9.3 *Premium calculation* – the pure risk premium will be based on the level of risk the insured brings to the insurer. However, the actual premium quoted also takes into account a number of other factors:

- *The need to create a reserve sufficient to cope with unpredicted occurrences/ claims.*
- *Meeting the insurance company's expenses.*
- *Making a contribution to the insurance company's profits.*
- *The current and predicted future rates of investment return and inflation.*
- *Insurance premium tax at the required rate which is payable to the Customs and Excise.*
- *What other insurers are quoting for similar risks.*

9.4 Once the proposer has confirmed that the insurance can commence a policy document is issued. The insurer also arranges to collect premiums from the insured person either by cheque or direct debit.

The insurer will also take care of the annual renewal notice in time to ensure that premium payment is continuous and the insured does not inadvertently forget to re-insure themselves. Normally they won't be asked to complete a new proposal form, just confirm that there have been no material changes.

9.5   There are some obvious benefits to customers of general insurance. These benefits are generally related to peace of mind, for the following reasons:

- *Because they will be happy that there will be some financial security in the event of loss or damage.*
- *In the case of car insurance they will be compliant with the law and if there is a serious accident then their insurance company can help sort this out if third-party claims are involved.*
- *A number of insurers will take the hassle out of sorting out claims and payment for replacement goods.*

10.0
Non-regulated products

Traditionally, there have been a number of products and services offered by the financial service providers that have not been regulated by the Financial Services Act 1986, but by different legislation. As well as general insurance, these are cheque and savings accounts, personal lending and credit cards. As such, non-authorised staff were able to sell and give advice on these products.

10.1   *Cheque and savings accounts* – savings accounts were dealt with in section 7.1 and we will now take a look at cheque or current accounts.

People have a basic need for a bank account for receipt of wages and a means of paying for goods and services. It's safer than having lots of cash around the house and is useful to pay for bills by direct debit and standing orders. There is the convenience factor with the use of debit and credit cards.

Having this basic platform gives customers access to other financial services, which they may need at some point in their lives, such as personal loans, mortgages and investment products.

Customers like to be able to access their funds and information about their account in a variety of different ways. This can be by cash machine, branch, call centre, the Internet or mobile phone, whichever way they chose there are enough ways to give them 24-hour a day coverage, 365 days per year. They can receive regular statements and cheque books as standard services.

There are many of different packages offered by the financial services providers which in many cases are tailored to suit different people and their lifestyles. In addition to the standard current account there are accounts for:

- *Under 19's.*
- *Students.*
- *Graduates.*

These accounts are designed to build loyalty and to gain customers when they are new to banking. Additional lifestyle accounts include:

- *Budget accounts.*
- *Accounts for people on higher incomes who have a relationship manager and additional services.*

Note

What different types of current accounts does your organisation offer to customers?

There is obviously lots of competition between the financial services providers to obtain new current accounts. They often offer good deals to new customers in the form of low overdraft rates and commission-free services on travel money. However, many of the accounts on offer have very similar features and benefits and those that are different are soon easily copied. This can become very confusing for customers when trying to find what is the best product for them.

Note

What does your organisation offer that you feel is different from other financial services providers?

Organisations can differentiate themselves through superior levels of service, convenience, such as the supermarkets have done, or through an ethical stance such as the Co-operative Bank or by the power of a trusted brand, such as Virgin Direct.

There is a large amount of information that can be collected when accounts opened and many organisations will do credit reference check before opening the account to satisfy themselves of the credit history. Approximately 25% of customers' accounts are a cost to the organisation so it is important from the organisation's point of view that they minimise the risk of taking on an account that will be costly to maintain. Also there is a cost to opening a new account and whilst it is necessary to attract customers, from a business perspective good customers are more profitable and worth retaining.

Note

What does your organisation do to encourage customer loyalty?

By opening a current account not only does the customer have access to other goods and services provided, that organisation has more opportunity to cross-sell products and services to the customer. This means there is more opportunity for income from this customer. It is also thought that the more products the customer holds with a particular provider the more loyal they are likely to be.

11.0

Personal lending

As we have seen above, opening a bank account gives the customer access to the possibility of borrowing money from the financial services provider. One way of doing this is by mortgage (see section 8) where the lender has the security of a legal charge over the customer's home. Customers may then borrow further money lent against the security of their home, if there is sufficient equity available.

There are two further types of borrowing that customers may take. These may or may not be regulated by the Consumer Credit Act 1974, which will be discussed in detail in Unit 4.

11.1 *Overdrafts* – an overdraft is a form of short-term temporary borrowing offered by financial service providers. The purpose of an overdraft is to help the customer over a period in which their expenditure may exceed their income. For personal customers this may be when they have outgoings needed to be paid for before receipt of their wages or bonus. This can be by a permanent arrangement whereby the customer has an agreed overdraft limit placed on their account. The amount of this limit will depend on such factors as their monthly income, the way they run their account and how long they have held their account. This will cover normal day-to-day fluctuations in spending and income.

The other way to run an overdraft is to have an agreed limit, which is for a set, short-term period only and will be covered by receipt of specific money that repay it. As the agreement is for a fixed period only, there may be a need for them to re-negotiate this limit at the end of the period if the money has not come through as expected.

These 'agreed' overdrafts are normally a relatively inexpensive form of borrowing and are a good way for customers to cover short-term shortfalls in income. The danger is that the customer never gets their account back into credit and develops a 'hardcore' of borrowing which they never manage to repay. At this point they would be advised to consider moving this amount onto a loan account, which will be discussed next.

'Unauthorised' overdrafts are those where the customer either inadvertently or deliberately goes overdrawn without advising their financial services provider that they are going to do so. This type of borrowing is penalised by charging the customer a much higher rate of interest. This can be the cause of many customer complaints, when the error was accidental, so causing unnecessary charges and interest. A number of financial services providers offer free overdrafts for a set number of days up to a set limit, on their accounts to try to avoid this.

Note

What is the difference in interest rates between the 'agreed' overdraft interest rate and the 'unauthorised' interest rate from your organisation?

11.2 *Personal loans* – loans are for more long-term purposes, such as consolidation of overdrafts or credit card debts onto one account, for car purchase or paying for holidays. This gives the customer peace of mind knowing they have one figure to pay each month with an end date in sight.

Many financial services providers have centralised the assessment of applications by using a credit scoring system, which is controlled by the organisation's lending function, to assess the suitability of a borrower. Much research goes into the models to create these systems, however, they will only be as reliable as the information given by the customer. Some financial services providers are able to 'pre-sanction' loans and overdrafts and this information can be stored on the customer's account details and made available to them when they ask for it. This speeds up time when a customer needs assistance.

Personal loans are usually unsecured loans where the lender relies on the borrower's promise to repay. This makes the loans a higher risk for the lender and as such the maximum term allowed for this type of loan will be shorter – typically eight to ten years. For the same reason they will tend to attract higher interest rates. Most personal loans will be on a fixed interest rate over a fixed term, and, therefore, not subject to variations in changes in base rate.

> **Note**
>
> Compare the interest rate between your organisation's mortgage rate, overdraft rate and personal loan account rate.

The purpose of the loan, up to a figure of £25,000, determines whether it is regulated by the Consumer Credit Act 1974. If related to house purchase or home improvements, for example, it is exempt.

12.0
Credit cards, debit cards and charge cards

Another range of products that can be offered to a new customer are plastic cards. Since their introduction in the UK in the early 1970s, these cards have become a familiar part of everyday life. Credit and debit cards are an extremely convenient way to buy goods and services and have led to a considerable reduction in the use of cash and cheques. They are acceptable almost everywhere globally, some countries even accepting them for very small payments such as on buses or in taxis.

They come in a number of different forms:

12.1   *Credit cards* – as well as providing cash-free purchasing convenience, credit cards are a source of 'revolving credit'. The customer has a credit limit and can use the card for purchases or other transactions up to that amount provided that at least a specified minimum amount (usually 5% of the outstanding balance) is repaid each month.

Credit cards are an expensive way to borrow, with rates of interest considerably higher than most other lending products. That said many credit card promoters offer introductory rates for balances transferred from other providers. There also tend to be charges for obtaining cash on the credit card.

There are two main credit card companies operating worldwide. Most credit cards issued in the UK are branded to financial services organisations, building societies, retail stores, clubs and societies. However, they are basically either Visa or Master-Card. There are exceptions to this, one of which is Marks and Spencer, which runs its own credit card through a subsidiary finance company.

Credit card companies charge a fee to the retailers for their service. This is deducted as a percentage of the value of the transactions when the credit card company makes settlement to the retailer. For this reason you will sometimes see a small charge added or a minimum amount transaction for purchases made by credit card.

12.2   *Charge cards* – although used by the customer in the same way as a credit card to make purchases, the outstanding balance on a charge card account must be paid in full at the end of the month. The best-known example of this is American Express.

12.3   *Debit cards* – these are an innovation introduced in the late 1980s and examples are Switch, Delta and Connect. They enable cardholders to make electronic payments directly from their cheque account to the account of the retailer. The system effectively replaces the use of cheques and in the long-term should reduce the costs involved of processing this type of transaction.

12.4   *Electronic purse* – a recent innovation originally introduced for piloting in the UK in 1995 by a consortium company (of UK Banks) known as Mondex. This system enables customers to make purchases using a 'smart card', which is a plastic card that has a computer chip embedded in it, rather than a magnetic strip on the back. The card can be topped up with electronic cash direct from the customer's account over the telephone using a specially adapted terminal. The card was meant for small transactions that normally require lots of coins, so making it a more convenient method of payment for customers and retailers.

The idea has not really taken off in the UK, however other places such as Hong Kong, South and North America have seen more successful launches and usage. MasterCard now holds the controlling interest in Mondex, rather than the UK banks and other uses are being developed, such as including security passes and loyalty schemes on the same card.

13.0
Other intermediaries and advice for customers

From what you have studied so far it will be clear that the vast array of financial services products is not only very complex but also changing at a very rapid place. It is not surprising that members of the public should feel that they need the advice and guidance of professionals to find their way through the financial jungle. This might be deciding what type of current account or savings account is right for them, all the way through to the right mortgage and life assurance policies. Many of these decisions often involve large amounts of money over long periods and need to be thought through carefully.

Fortunately there is plenty of help available and the work of the regulatory body means that customers should only receive advice from suitably knowledgeable and skilled practitioners. It is important that customers know where they can go for this advice and that they should be made aware of any potential limitations to the advice they are given.

We have already looked at what customers can expect from a financial services organisation. Let us now look at some of the other sources where they can obtain advice. This will come from the professionals who, either as an integral or incidental part of their role, give advice on financial matters to their customers. If they give investment advice they need to be authorised under the terms of the FSMA 2000. Professional firms carrying on mainstream investment business will be directly regulated by the FSA to ensure that they meet comparable standards to those applicable to other businesses in the investment community. Other professional firms, which do not carry on mainstream investment business, will not be regulated by the FSA. These are firms where:

- *The regulated activity is provided in an incidental manner in the course of a professional activity.*
- *The activity is subordinate to the main professional services which the firm provides.*
- *The firm does not offer regulated activities as a separate service.*
- *The firm does not receive payment for the service other than from its customer.*

An example of non-mainstream activity might be where a solicitor sells shares on the instructions of an executor of a will without giving advice. However, if that solicitor engaged in an activity relating to a 'sensitive' product such as mortgage-related endowment policies this may be considered as mainstream.

This is an area that the FSA is going to keep under review and if it was considered necessary to regulate this area directly to protect consumers then it would do so.

These differing sources of advice present other forms of competition to financial service providers and it may be that customers have their own trusted advisers that they use for varying purposes. Wherever possible, customer contact staff need to ensure that they can build relationships with customers so that they feel that they would prefer to stay with the organisation rather than take their business elsewhere. It is important for you to understand what the role of these different firms are and what products and services they can provide.

13.1   *Insurance brokers* – many insurance brokers deal only in general insurance and, therefore, do not have to be authorised under the FSA. If they transact life assurance and pensions business authorisation is required.

13.2   *Accountants* – for many self-employed people and small business owners their accountant is the main regular point of contact regarding financial matters. It is, therefore, not surprising that accountants are often asked for advice on pensions, insurance and investments. If this advice is part of the mainstream services offered then authorisation will be required.

13.3   *Solicitors* – investment advice is incidental to a number of aspects of solicitor's work. For example:

- *Preparation of a client's will may lead to discussion of inheritance tax liabilities and of the ways in which life assurance policies could be used to mitigate the effects of this tax.*
- *Dealing with the distribution of a deceased client's estate could lead to the beneficiaries enquiring on how best to invest their legacies.*
- *Acting for a client who is purchasing a house may involve a solicitor in the business of obtaining or repaying a mortgage and the associated assurance and insurance policies.*

Again, if the activities are considered to be mainstream then the solicitors' firm will require authorisation from the FSA.

13.4   *Estate agents* – although it is not essential to use the services of an estate agent in order to buy or sell a property the majority of people do so. Every sale provides the estate agent with contacts which could lead to the sale of financial services products of various kinds. For example, many estate agents are able to offer to assist purchasers obtain a mortgage, however, if they wish to give advice on possible repayment vehicles for interest only mortgages then they need to be authorised by the FSA. Most estate agents ask whether clients already have mortgage facilities arranged when they wish to view a property, as they are looking for opportunities to arrange or advise on this service themselves. This means a financial services provider has to be very quick to get there first or have a high degree of existing loyalty from their customers.

Recognition of the opportunity to 'cross-sell' financial products in the late 1980s led to many financial institutions moving into the estate agency market, through the purchase of existing agencies. This proved to be a painful experience for many organisations with cross-selling proving to be much more difficult to achieve than had been anticipated. The situation was compounded by the downturn in the housing market resulting in many organisations cutting their losses and pulling out. There are, however, one or two more successful names on the high street such as the Halifax and the Bradford and Bingley.

13.5 *Stockbroking and share dealing* – investors can deal in shares through agency brokers (stockbrokers) and financial services organisations. Local stockbrokers are very good at building relationships with their clients and are able to retain their business for many years. The share dealing departments of organisations are able to give advice to clients on the selection of share and timing of purchases and sales and can be supported by advisers that build relationships with customers at a local level. This advice is governed by the FSA and again the advisers should be authorised individuals.

Unit 3

Identifying the key issues affecting personal financial services markets

The aim of this module is to enable you to outline and explain:

- *The competitive forces from new entrants, suppliers, customers and switching to substitutes.*
- *The emergence of new distribution channels and increasing rate of change.*
- *Consumer habits and demands, social factors and changes in demographics.*
- *The strength of suppliers and resource issues for financial services organisations.*
- *Government policies and the implications for customers and organisations.*

In Unit 1, we looked at the macro-economic environment and the forces which affected it. There were some key influences that were:

- *Political/legal.*
- *Sociocultural.*
- *Technological.*
- *Economic.*

We also looked at customer needs and how organisations can meet these needs. Unit 2 dealt with regulation through the Financial Services and Markets Act 2000 and how this affects products, how they are sold and by whom.

This section seeks to make the link between the changing needs of the consumer over their lifestages and the changing environment in which people live. This changing environment is affected by the macro-economic factors above, which in turn can bring about changes in people's lives and behaviour.

Examples of this are:

- *Political/legal – changes in car tax as a result of emissions regulation has made some consumers consider what car they might buy.*
- *Sociocultural – the growth of organic food production and consumption as a result of food scares.*
- *Technological – the growth of mobile phones with their variety of uses.*
- *Economic – reduction of interest rates giving an increase in disposable income to be spent on other things.*

It is a very dynamic environment with a high rate of change. Organisations can be reactive in this environment, where they follow consumer demand, or proactive. This is where they attempt to anticipate customer needs or are able to create a need as a result of the environmental change. An example of this would be Amazon, who very successfully anticipated the need for, and sold, books over the Internet.

1.0
Competitive forces

The success of an organisation will depend on how well it can cope with the competition. Measurement of success is often talked about in terms of market share, such as a percentage of the personal customer base or mortgage lending market for example. Organisations are often under pressure to perform in these areas and watch very closely the activities of those they perceive to be competitor organisations.

There are, however, other factors, not just the other organisations that offer similar products, which affect this. These other factors are the customers themselves, the suppliers, potential newcomers to the market and substitute products. These can be seen as competitive pressure too. This is because the actions of these other groups can affect the organisation's fortunes in quite a dramatic way.

The role of the organisation's senior management is to find a place in the industry which proves the best defence against all the competitive factors, or to be able to have a positive influence over it. The departments and teams in the organisation all have their role in making their plans for this come to fruition.

1.1 Threat of entry from potential newcomers

Figure 3.1 shows a diagrammatical representation of the forces on the competitive environment.

Taking each of these in turn, potential newcomers to the environment bring increased capacity, which means that over-supply of products and service can result. This means an increased choice for customers and, if the product offering

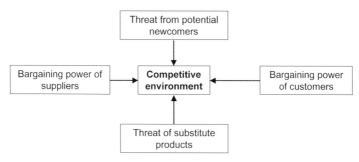

Figure 3.1 *The competitive environment adapted from Michael E Porter.*

is new, innovative or represents value for money, there is a likelihood that customers will switch to the new provider. This will be detrimental to organisations that are already supplying the market. These newcomers also have a high drive to gain market share and can amass large resources to help them.

Potential newcomers for the financial services providers have come in recent years from a number of places such as:

- *Banks moving into areas where building societies once dominated and vice versa.*
- *Retailers, such as supermarkets and high street stores, providing financial services along with their goods.*
- *Insurance companies diversifying into banking and mortgage lending to compliment existing activities.*
- *Foreign banks looking to increase their global presence such as HSBC's (Hong Kong and Shanghai Bank) takeover of Midland Bank.*

How serious this threat is to the existing organisations can depend on a number of factors:

- *Economies of scale – if a large infrastructure is required, then it is difficult to set up a new company. The retailers and insurance companies have worked in partnership with existing providers for the provision of their products and have overcome this obstacle.*
- *Product differentiation – where the products are similar, such as in financial services, it is difficult to be different from the competition. This is where having a strong brand is useful. Virgin were able to attract new customers because of the strength of the brand from the successful image of Richard Branson and his other businesses. Egg was able to differentiate itself as an innovative Internet bank and First Direct has been able to differentiate itself as the first to deliver good customer service over the telephone.*
- *Capital requirements – usually a new venture requires large amounts of cash to*

launch. An investment in a new financial services organisation will be great and limits the number of likely newcomers.

- *Access to distribution channels – distribution channels are the methods by which an organisation reaches its customers. This can be via branches, shops, the Internet or a call/contact centre. The supermarkets and high street retailers had a ready-made distribution channel and cash was available in the tills should customers wish draw this from their accounts. Many existing financial services organisations have large branch networks, which have become a high overhead and have resulted in a number of closure programmes that have been very unpopular with customers. The success of direct banking through call/contact centres and the Internet have shown that a physical presence on the high street is not necessary for success. The changing requirements of the customers for higher accessibility to information has pushed this area of change.*

- *Government policies and regulation – the financial services industry has become highly regulated (covered fully in Unit 4) and is a very important part of any organisation and individual operating in this field. Newcomers to this industry have to show that they can comply with the regulations that protect customers and employees.*

The high rate of change has been increased by the relatively easy entrance of these newcomers to the financial services industry.

1.2   Bargaining power of suppliers and customers

In terms of 'suppliers' these can be customers themselves as they provide cash balances on which financial organisations may depend on to lend to other customers (Unit 1, section 3). If the suppliers are not happy with the interest rate they are receiving for their balances, they can shop around until they find a better rate. This is notwithstanding that there may be other features and benefits about their deposit account or levels or service, which means they are prepared to accept a lower interest rate.

Note

What are the other supplies do financial services organisations use in their day-to-day activities?

What would be the effect if some of these materials were not available?

Consider the effects of the fuel crisis and protests in 2000. Many people were not able to travel long distances because they had limited supplies of petrol. The effect on businesses and the country as a whole would have been very dramatic if this problem had continued for a long period of time.

In summary, suppliers are only powerful if:

- *They are dominated by a few major players – as in the fuel crisis.*
- *The product is unique or different – such as when First Direct was launched.*
- *The supplier is important to the industry – can they do without them? If large numbers of customers were to close their accounts and move to another provider, this would be highly detrimental to the organisation's ability to lend within the guidelines laid down.*

The power of customers will be high where:

- *There are large volume buyers – personal customers individually tend not to be that powerful because the amount they contribute to the total income of the organisation is relatively small. Corporate customers however may be more powerful depending on their size and relative importance. If, however, any customers collectively take action then this could be damaging for the organisation.*
- *Products are similar from each provider – this makes it easier for a customer to switch to a new provider because they know that they can get their needs met easily elsewhere. It is also easier for customers to play one provider off against the other to obtain a better deal. The John Lewis partnership try to overcome this by their motto 'never knowingly undersold' which is to show people they can get the best deal with their store.*
- *The product does not save the buyer money – when the product does save money for the customer, they will be happier to pay a premium for it and be more interested in the quality of what they receive. An example would be the Dyson vacuum cleaner, which, over time, saves money on buying new bags. Where the product does not save money the customer will be less willing to pay a high price and be more likely to look for the best deal they can. This is why customers will spend time looking for good interest rates for saving and borrowing.*

Note

How much power does the average personal financial services customer have when purchasing products?

> How can financial services organisations make products more attractive to customers?

The average personal financial services customer has power in that there is a similar choice from many providers and many of these products do not necessarily save them money. This means that they will be looking for other benefits, such as good service, accessibility and convenience.

1.3 The final competitive pressure is the threat of substitute products. Examples of this are e-mail replacing the postal service, mobile phones replacing land-lines, CDs replacing vinyl records and personal data assistants replacing the pocket diary. This limits the profitability of the original product, however, more importantly it changes the way people run their lives, their behaviour and habits.

Think

Think about the following questions:

> How would the office environment change if there were no PCs just manual typewriters?
>
> How would people cope at home if they had to go back to using a tub and mangle rather than a washing machine?
>
> Candles are fashionable at the moment, what would it be like if we had to use them all the time instead of electricity?

In the financial services environment there have been some interesting developments, which show how effective substitute products can be:

- *In the 1980s 'free banking' was introduced by the then Midland Bank (now HSBC Group). This was previously unheard of. This bold step, which threatened* to lead to a mass migration of accounts from the other banks to Midland, sent shock waves throughout the industry. Within weeks the other banks were also offering free banking. This has become the norm today.

- The HSBC Group struck again with the launch of the first telephone contact centre 'First Direct' in October 1989. This substitute for branch banking did cause a rapid outflow of accounts from other financial services providers. First Direct soon gained an enviable reputation for good customer service and remains successful today. Many organisations now offer contact centre banking as a substitute to branch banking and for customers this is an accepted way of doing business.

2.0
New distribution channels and rates of change

2.1 We have already commented on changing distribution channels in Unit 1, and how the branch network of many of the retail financial services organisations has been supplemented by contact centres and Internet sites. There are two main ways in which the need for a new distribution channel is identified:

- By surveying the customers in the marketplace – an example of this is First Direct (mentioned in 1.3). As part of the initial project research was done, by independent bodies, to find out what people thought about branch banking. MORI research found that:
  - 20% of people had not visited their branch in the last 12 months.
  - 51% people said they would rather visit their branch as little as possible.
  - 48% had never met their branch manager.
  - 27% wished they were able to conduct more business over the telephone.
  The Henley Centre for Forecasting found that:
  - consumer demand for better service was higher amongst banks than any other retail sector;
  - friendly knowledgeable staff were considered important; and
  - customers wanted convenient opening hours and easy transactions
  This led to the conclusion that a new bank was required that offered round-the-clock, direct access.
  NatWest (now part of the Royal Bank of Scotland Group) had previously come to the same conclusion and had launched a central telephone service known as 'Cashwise'. This, however, had a low take-up from customers, which could have been for a variety of reasons such as insufficient telephone technology, advertising and product range, or just that customers did not feel ready to conduct their banking over the phone. This service was eventually closed down. This failure

shows that the external environment has to be right for new distribution channels to work effectively and customers need to feel comfortable to switch to new ways of doing business.

- *New product innovation – the pro-active method of creating a new distribution channel is for organisations to artificially create need in the minds of their customers. An example of this is satellite TV, where TV service is transmitted digitally to a decoder rather than by the conventional method of terrestrial TV. This method allows add-on services such as home shopping. This approach usually needs heavy marketing and advertising to make it successful. What also tends to happen is that new products, that may at first appear functional, such as satellite TV and mobile phones, soon become fashionable and the next upgrade becomes a 'must have'. This is of course dependent upon how successful the product is. For example, WAP phones have not been as good as first envisaged so have not become widely used.*

    An example of new product innovation in financial services was the Virgin One Account. At the time of its launch many of the financial services commentators were concerned that it would not be prudent for customers to use such an account, which combined their current account and their mortgage. However, it was a clear way in which customers could effectively save money and soon has become very popular.

It would appear that in financial services customers are becoming more open to different ways of doing business that are no longer the traditional accepted methods. Whilst there is a place for face-to-face advice much can be done via alternative means.

2.2   This rate of change seems to be constantly accelerating and is highly dependent upon the external political, economic, socio-cultural and technological factors. These have been referred to in the introduction to this module and also in the introduction to Unit 1.

Note

To recap:

What are some of the main political factors in the environment that can affect customers?

What are some of the economic factors that affect customers?

What might be some of the socio-cultural factors affecting customers?

How does technology affect the way organisations deliver their services?

For a review of this topic area please return to the introduction of Unit 1 if required.

When considering the changes an organisation needs to make to meet these external demands and customer preferences, the management can use a SWOT analysis to help determine what they need to do. The organisation's internal strengths and weaknesses are plotted along with the external opportunities and threats. Customer feedback is particularly useful during this exercise.

Once a course of action has been identified and evaluated the change programme can be put into place. There are two types of change as in Figure 3.2.

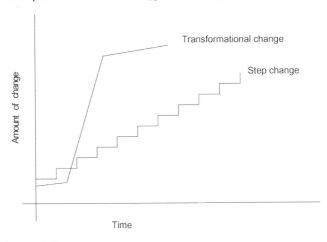

Figure 3.2 *Types of change.*

- *Transformational change – this type of change requires lots of effort, it is costly, high risk and often a new venture. If successful it can have a high impact. An example of this is when Prudential Insurance launched Egg, providing Financial Services over the Internet. This was something very new and consumers saw a big difference immediately.*

- *Step change – this type of change requires smaller amounts of effort over a longer period. It is lower risk and less expensive in the short term. If the change is happening within an organisation, it may require cultural change within the organisation to get people to do things differently. This can be the hardest part for an organisation to manage. Customers may not see or appreciate the difference, and indeed it is hard to influence the customers' perceptions when the changes are smaller. An example of this is the reduction of the use of physical cash and the increase of electronic methods of payment.*

Think

Consider the following:

What sort of change has happened within your organisation?

How was this managed?

How long did it take for the changes to become 'the norm'?

Note

How are changes about products and services communicated to customers?

How effective are these methods?

As you have probably already thought, communication is key to any change process. In order to manage change effectively both inside and outside the organisation's employees need to keep their knowledge up-to-date and communicate well.

There are, however, barriers to change both within organisations and from the customers themselves:

Note

What stops change happening within your organisation?

Think of a time when you have been a customer and you have received information about a change to product or service.
Did you consider the change to be beneficial?

If not, what were your objections to the change?

Barriers to change within organisations typically are:

- *Complacency about the necessity for change from individuals and the organisation and a general feeling of inertia.*
- *Individuals feel they are being marginalised or made worse off by the changes and so resist the changes.*
- *Lack of information about what is happening and where the change is going to take people and the business.*
- *Fear of the unknown and people being asked to operate outside 'comfort zones'.*
- *Historical or traditional reasons and a wish to do things the way they have always been done.*

Barriers to change from customers are broadly similar and can be summarised as:

- *Apathy – they do not wish to change and are happy with the status quo.*

- *Loyalty – they feel emotionally attached to their service or product provider. People tend to trust what they know and what has worked in the past.*
- *Fear – they do not wish to enter into the unknown and feel apprehensive about doing so.*
- *Lack of understanding – the changes may appear complex in the way that they have been communicated, which adds to the customers' reluctance to change.*

It is the role of the organisation and its employees, therefore, to manage both the internal change and the external changes the customers experience. As we have seen some of these changes there is a degree of control over and some of which that are driven by factor outside our control. Helping customers to understand and manage these changes every time products or services are updated is a key role to be fulfilled.

3.0
Consumer habits and demands

We have looked at the external environment from a business perspective, however, we also need to look at what has been happening within the population. Research is carried out around social trends by the government each year, which can be used by politicians, councillors and business people to try to help them forecast how best to meet the needs of the population. Areas researched include:

- *Population profile.*
- *Households and families.*
- *Income and wealth.*
- *Expenditure.*
- *Housing.*
- *The environment.*
- *Lifestyles and social participation.*

There are other reports prepared on such matters as share ownership, the labour market, health and care and crime and justice. Organisations also can have reports prepared by internal or external researchers for marketing or planning purposes.

This information helps build a picture of what consumer habits are, what their demands are likely to be and the changes in demographics (the make up of the population). These changes affect what, and how much, particular products and services are likely to be taken up. We looked at people's life-stages in Unit 1 and how these affect the types of products and services that are suitable for them over their lifetime.

In the First Direct example used in sections 1 and 2 we looked at how research helped inform the decision to set up the telephone bank. It was subsequently found, from surveying the new customer base, that the typical customer that was attracted to the service was aged between 25–44 (71% of total First Direct customer base) and an early adopter of new technology. These people tended to come from the more affluent parts of society. Looking at social trends further would help First Direct tailor their products and services for their customer base.

3.1   Population profile – consider these statistics from 1999 about the population of the UK:

- It was estimated to be 59.5 million, 20th largest in the world. Compare this with 1851 when the population was 22.3 million.
- Just over a quarter of the people were aged under 20, compared with just under half in 1821.
- 16% of people were aged 65 or over compared with approximately 7% in 1821.

Think

> What does this tell you about the age profile of the population in the UK today?

The population is increasing and 'ageing', this means that there have been reductions in mortality rates for older people and lower fertility rates in younger people. Projections suggest these trends will continue, so that by 2016 the number of people aged 65 and over will exceed those aged under 16. This profile is not just something peculiar to the UK. Other European countries are similar, with the exception of the Irish Republic, who has the lowest proportion of the 65 and over age group, a figure that has remained steady since 1960.

Another factor on the age of the population is the number of people migrating to and from the country. This inflow of people was highest just after the Second World War, however this was curtailed in the 1960s and 1970s. In general, ethnic minority groups have a younger age structure than the white population, however progressive ageing of this sector of the population is anticipated in the future.

Another interesting feature of the population profile is by gender and social class. Figure 3.3 shows a breakdown of population of working age by gender and social class:

United Kingdom

Percentages

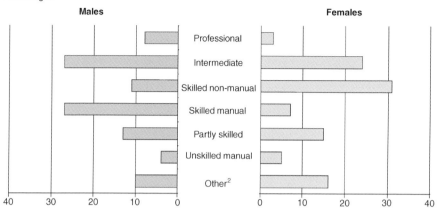

1 Males aged 16 to 64, females aged 16 to 59.
2 Includes members of the armed forces, those who did not state their current or last occupation and those who had not worked in the last eight years.
Source: Labour Force Survey, Office for National Statistics

Figure 3.3 *Population of working age by gender and social class.*

In spring of 2000 men of working age were three times more likely than women to be in professional occupations. Women were more likely to be in the skilled non-manual group. This reflects the number of women in occupations such as clerical roles and the increasing participation of women in the workforce. The number of women moving into professional roles is gradually increasing.

Another factor is where people live in the UK. This can be quite difficult to track over time, however, records do show that London has always contained the highest density of people, whilst the Highlands of Scotland have always had the lowest density. The population of the UK has been highly urbanised for much of the 20th century. By 1991 nearly 90% of people were living in urban areas. The largest area was London, the next largest being the metropolitan counties of the West Midlands and Manchester.

Added to this is how many people move from region to region, and to and from the UK. This has implications for local land use, housing planning and the provision of welfare services. In 1999 the greatest fall in the population was in London where 65,000 people left to move to other regions within the UK. This was offset by the inflow of migrants into the capital. The South-West experienced the highest net gain of all the regions caused by internal migration of 33,000 people.

Think

What does all this mean for consumers?

The effects of these factors can be summarised as:

- *An ageing population means that provision for people in their old age will become more important. This could be in terms of healthcare, income after retirement and suitable housing. However the usual way of providing many services to the 'retireds' is by government from taxes and if the number of young people in work and paying taxes is falling, then meeting this cost becomes a problem.*
- *The number of women with their own income is increasing, they become financially independent, being able to fit in their working role with childcare. It may be that they become the biggest income earner in the family. There may well be a number of women changing job situations over their lifetime – a full-time role, having time out for a family, returning to a full-time or part-time role or perhaps multiple part-time roles.*
- *The demand for housing outside London is increasing, young families wish to move to somewhere that has better facilities for children than an inner city. This then means a requirement to commute to their place of work. This means more house building and an increase in the communications infrastructure.*

Think

How might financial services providers take advantage of this opportunities?

To take advantage of these opportunities financial services providers could:

- *Advise people of the need to increase their pension provisions – education of both personal and business customers about this is important. It is likely that, in the future, the state pension will be insufficient for most people's old age. The recently launched stakeholder pension is aimed at raising awareness of this need and providing everyone a chance to do this, whether they are in employment or not. There is a real need to ensure that people consider their pension provision from an early age so they can take the maximum time available to pay into it. There is also a need to allow retired people to release the equity in their property to supplement their income and a financial vehicle to do this.*
- *Aim flexible financial services products at women and other carers who have a changing work pattern.*

- *Market mortgages focusing on the type of people who are moving out of London to these other areas.*

3.2 Households and families – as we have seen the population of the UK has increased dramatically during the 20th century. The number of households has tripled over the same period. Almost 30% of households comprised of one person living alone in 2000, this is two-and-a-half times as many as in 1960. This is not just young people living alone but the elderly too.

The projected numbers per household is expected to fall over time. This is due to the decline in marriage, the rise of separation and divorce, as well as people marrying at older ages. The number of co-habiting couples has doubled since the 1960s.

The average age of women having children in England and Wales rose from 26.2 years in 1971, to 29 in 1999. The trend is also for smaller families:

- *In 1972, 41% of 'couple' families had three or more children.*
- *In 2000 this figure was 26%.*

These changes in the country's population and structure, their values and in social legislation, have affected the characteristics of the traditional view of family and households. The biggest life changes within families are the birth and departure of children and the adjustments experienced when joining a new partner.

Think

How might financial service providers assist with these sorts of life changes and changes in the population?

To assist with these life changes and changes in the population financial services organisations could:

- *Increase products related to home ownership – this could be by way of mortgages and insurance. Moving house is one of the most stressful experiences people have in life, so providing friendly advice and an efficient service at this time would be very welcome from a customer perspective.*
- *Link products to children's lifestage events – this could be in the form of savings or insurance for a particular event.*

3.3 The effect home of home ownership – during the last two centuries the number of dwellings in the UK increased substantially from nearly two million from the start of the 19th century, to nearly 25 million at the start of the 21st century. This increase was encouraged by deregulation in planning and the building industry and also the legislation in 1980, which allowed council tenants to buy their own homes. Between 1981 and 2000 the number of owner occupied dwellings in the UK increased by more than 40 per cent. The number of homes rented from a Registered Social Landlord more than doubled over the same period.

Approximately, 20 per cent of dwellings in England were built before the end if the First World War and almost 40 per cent since 1965. The type of house was also changing. Larger detached and semi-detached houses were preferred to the pre-war terrace housing. There was an aspiration to purchase largest house people could afford, regardless of family size or household.

Life-cycle changes appear to relate to tenure (whether rented or owner occupied) of property. In 1999–2000:

- Almost half of households headed by people under 25 were living in privately rented accommodation – far greater than any other age group.
- Heads of households over 65 were most likely to own their property outright and many would have repaid their mortgage by the time they retired.
- It is expected that over time more people will become owner-occupiers.

Attitudes to home ownership vary according to the housing market and economy. When interest rates rose and economic recession set in 1989, attitudes to home

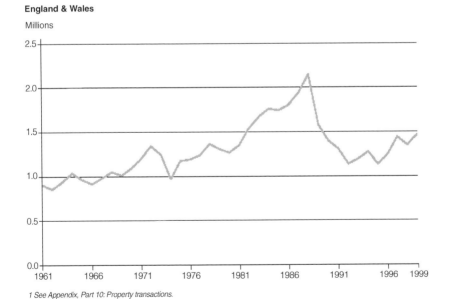

England & Wales

Millions

1 See Appendix, Part 10: Property transactions.

Source: Inland Revenue

Figure 3.4 *Property transactions.*

ownership became less favourable. Attitudes do not appear to have responded entirely to the subsequent economic upturn and are now less positive towards some aspects of home ownership. In saying this, the number of property transactions has increased from the low of 1991 and appears to follow the cycles of economic growth and recession.

In 1999 the average price of a dwelling in England and Wales was £94,600. The popularity of the endowment mortgage continued to decline, following a number of endowment policies poor performance in the late 1990s. 83 per cent of houses were purchased with an endowment in 1988 compared with 27 per cent in 1999.

Think

> What do these figures about housing mean for the provision of mortgages by financial service providers?

Bearing these figures in mind financial service providers can:

- *Ensure that people do not overstretch themselves in terms of being able to afford the mortgage repayments, and make sure people have budgeted for increases in unforeseen costs and interest rates. One way to help here is to offer fixed interest rate mortgages.*
- *Review the performance of endowment policies when they support mortgage repayment to ensure that there will be sufficient funds to repay the mortgage at the end of the term. Alternative risk-free repayment methods are more likely to be appealing to consumers.*
- *Provide an efficient service for agreeing and processing mortgage applications so that there is not undue delay.*
- *Offer specialist mortgage finance for properties that will be let by landlords as this also appears to be an area for growth.*
- *Provide advice on wills and inheritance tax planning, as retired people need to ensure that they had made provision to dispose of any of property in the most tax efficient way.*

3.4   Share ownership – at the end of 2000 individuals' Stock market shareholdings amounted to £290 billion or 16 per cent of the total market. Levels of share ownership have been steadily decreasing since 1964, when individuals held 54 per cent of the market. However, this is not the complete picture as in 2000 individuals also held 37.2 per cent of investment trust shares – the largest percentage of this type investment owned by any one group. This shows that individuals prefer to spread their risk by using an investment trust that is more cost and time effective than trying to manage portfolios of shares themselves.

This is an opportunity for financial services institutions if they can introduce low-risk, low-maintenance investment products that are easy to understand and provide the individual peace of mind.

3.5   Customers have become better informed for a number of reasons:

- *Levels of education are better – there were 2.6 times as many people attending further and higher education in 1998/99 than in 1970/71. Not all of these people are school age; in Spring 2000 5.7 million people of working age were studying towards a qualification in the UK. Just over half were aged between 16–24. People with better education and the right sort of information and advice are more likely to be able to judge what they need successfully.*
- *Channels for obtaining information have increased. Consider the following figures from 1999–2000:*
  - *99% of households had television.*
  - *95% of households had a telephone.*
  - *38% of households had a home computer.*
  - *32% of households had satellite TV.*
- *People have become more sophisticated in their needs. Because of their changing lifestyles they need flexibility, as we have seen above.*
- *Increased competition across the financial services industry led to promise of service as a differentiator. This has led to higher levels of expectation from customers, who are more likely to complain and are often given the means to do so through customer surveys. Regulation has ensured that there are channels to do so through ombudsman bodies. The media is quick to point out deficiencies in products and services and, indeed, a number of TV programmes have made it their mission to do so.*
- *There is a general tendency for consumers to expect more for less. If people feel that a product is costing a significant amount of money they will want to see quality and value for money.*

This presents a significant challenge for organisations in the financial services sector.

> **Note**
>
> How does your organisation overcome these challenges?
>
>
> What else do you think your organisation could do to ensure customer satisfaction?

Organisations can employ a number of strategies to meet these customer challenges:

- *Promote well thought through products and services that meet the needs of the customers.*
- *Use of a number of distribution channels so that customers can access information about the products they hold and the products they want to know about.*
- *Good product and service literature, available in different media, brochures, the Internet and through well informed employees.*
- *Ensure that staff are fully trained and competent in the roles that they perform. This is a function of sound management practice and communication within the organisation.*
- *Put the customer first and have the ability to see issues from a customer's perspective.*

4.0
Suppliers and resourcing issues for financial services organisations

In section 1.2 we looked at the power of suppliers and customers and the effects if both of these parties are powerful on the competitive advantage of an organisation. In terms of the organisation, employees as a resource can be quite critical to the success of the organisation.

Consider the case of First Direct again:

- *When the organisation was set up, Leeds was chosen for the new site. This was because the rental rates were lower and the regional labour pool was used to lower salaries than in southern England.*

- The Yorkshire accent was recognised as easy to understand and considered warm and friendly.
- There was an availability of modern buildings in an industrial park outside Leeds that could be modified to suit the needs of the organisation. There was existing bank infrastructure which transactions could be processed through.
- Different 'people qualities' were required from that of traditional branch staff, who were seen as process orientated. These new qualities were:
  - Warm and engaging personalities, whilst being fast and efficient.
  - Empathy and responsiveness.
- By 1996 First Direct was the biggest private employer in Leeds, employing 2,400 people. By this time Leeds had become the hub of call centres in the UK for retailing, banking and utility companies. This made recruiting the right employees harder to do.
- Full training was given to new employees with the opportunity to change departments as their careers progressed. Pay was related to the individual and how their skills and knowledge developed with additional performance bonuses.
- The facilities reflected the twenty four hour working, such as:
  - A restaurant which was open from 7 a.m. to 9 p.m., seven days a week.
  - Free round the clock drinks from vending machines.
  - Day centres at two of the sites that looked after 150 small children.

Note

What were the resourcing issues for First Direct both initially and later in 1996?

How can organisations overcome some of these difficulties?

The resourcing issues can be summarised as follows:

- Cost of set-up and ongoing running costs in terms of employee salaries. The ongoing salary costs are the biggest ongoing costs.

- *Regional accents are important when determining where a central national location should be. They have to be acceptable to all callers as some accents are considered more trustworthy than others.*
- *There need to be suitable commercial properties available in sites where they is good transportation for employees to get to work.*
- *There has to be a pool of people who have the right attributes who can be employed. These people need to be more people orientated than process orientated. They can become high in demand if another employer opens a similar operation in the locality. It can be a problem if employees are lured away by better salaries or conditions.*
- *The fortunes of the community hinge on the success of a sole local employer who takes on large numbers of staff. The organisation has a social responsibility to that community. (See Unit 1, section 8.)*
- *New employees and those wishing career progression require training and development to be competent when dealing with customers. This is a large investment in the individual by the organisation and needs to be well managed.*
- *Matching pay and benefits to the needs of the employees is very important. As we have seen (section 3) a large proportion of the type of people employed in the call centre may well be women who prefer a flexible work pattern that they can match working around the needs of their family. Tailoring benefits around what their needs are is an important part of the salary package.*

In delivering the service to customers it would appear that there is a balancing act required to meet the needs of the organisation, the environment and the employees. The demographic patterns around the country will help inform organisations where the best sites might be.

Note

What would be the resource issues with setting up a contact centre site in central London?

The issues with setting up a contact centre site in London would be:

- *High costs both in terms of buildings and employment, costs due to higher costs in the south of England.*
- *There would be difficulties in finding a suitable building of the right size as new building land is not readily available in this area.*
- *It is likely that there would not be sufficient people with the right attributes to handle the type of work required. Once trained there would be a high possibility of them leaving to seek opportunities with the large number of other employers in the area.*

5.0
Government policies

Government polices, as already mentioned, impact on the external environment. These policies have implications for customers and organisations alike. The main legislation relating to the financial services sector will be discussed in Unit 4 in detail. As an introduction to that, let us look at some of the main ways in which government policy can be put into practice.

5.1 *Budget Day* – this is one of the key days in the parliamentary year. The Budget covers both the government's taxation plans for the coming fiscal year and its spending plans for the next three years. The details are announced by the Chancellor of the Exchequer in the House of Commons and are published in the 'Financial Statement and Budget report'.

Great secrecy surrounds the Budget and there is intense speculation in the run up to Budget day. There is considerable anticipation of the contents of the Chancellor's speech, which is broadcast on TV and radio and has much coverage in the press.

The announcement of the contents of the Budget releases a flood of information by the government. The major government departments put out news releases giving further details of the Chancellor's measures. This speech is then followed by a debate in Parliament on these measures.

Think

Consider this:

> Why do so many people show such interest in the contents of the Budget?

The Budget contains information that will affect people's disposable income. Those people paying tax will want to see if they will be paying more or less. Those on incomes controlled by government, such as pensioners, will want to see if their income has been increased. For organisations around the country, tax bands and rates of tax change along with National Insurance contributions, which affect payroll systems, which in turn impacts on their cashflow. These changes also can affect the financial advice given to customers when trying to take advantage of tax-free products.

5.2   *Acts of Parliament, Statutory Instruments and EU Legislation*

- *Acts of Parliament can be divided into two types – Public Acts and Private Acts. These are known as 'primary legislation'.*
  Public Acts are legislation of universal application and change general law. Private Acts (also known as Local and Personal Acts) affect the powers of individual groups, such as companies or local authorities.
    Most laws in the UK pass through Parliament as bills. When they have passed through all their stages these bills become Acts of Parliament. The debate around the bills is taken in various 'committees'. Some of the debate will involve The House of Commons and the House of Lords, e.g. bills of major constitutional importance or bills that need to be passed with unusual speed. There are also 'standing' committees and 'select' committees which are made up of individual MPs brought together to discuss specific topics and bills.
- *Statutory Instruments (SIs) are a form of legislation (often referred to as secondary legislation) which allow the provisions of an Act of Parliament to be subsequently brought into force or altered without Parliament having to pass a new Act.*
    An Act does not always regulate every detail of the subject it covers and there may be a number of such details in a very complicated Act. Also, an Act may specify details that subsequently need changing such as fees and time limits. Rather than pass a new Act every time these detailed changes to rules and regulations can be amended via a Statutory Instrument.
- *Most European community legislation requires UK legislation to supplement it before full implementation into English law. This may be effected by primary legislation (an Act) but is usually achieved by Statutory Instruments (secondary legislation).*

5.3   Ways of influencing legislation

- *Individuals can attempt to influence legislation in a number of ways. This may be by campaigns by the individual or in groups. This could involve petitions, protests or even legal action. They can try to influence their local MP and seek media backing to raise the profile of their argument.*

- *Organisations try to influence legislation by holding meetings with key figures to put their points across. This is called 'lobbying'. Members of Parliament have come under scrutiny in recent years for accepting payments for asking questions about specific topics during debates in Parliament. This is not a practice they are allowed to do and the scandal was aptly named 'cash for questions' by the press.*

Unit 4

Legislation that affects customer rights

The aim of this module is to enable you to outline the guidelines and legislation that affects customer rights, so that you can be aware of:

- *What legislation and guiding principles exist within the financial services sector.*
- *What customers rights are in certain situations and why.*
- *What you can and can not do in certain situations and why.*
- *What the implications are for you if you don't observe these guidelines and pieces of legislation.*

We have already looked at the Financial Services and Markets Act 2000 in some detail in Unit 2 and the remaining areas of importance will be covered here.

The study text has mentioned at various points how much regulation the financial services sector is governed by. This is in order to protect customers, staff and their organisations and minimise the risk of loss through a financial transaction. You will see that many of the procedures you follow are derived from this legislation in some way.

1.0
Customer relations

This section focuses on a number of areas that affect customer relations. Firstly there is the aspect of the legal contract set up between a customer and their financial service provider. This is usually done when an account is opened, which is why there are a number of checks that need to be carried out. Section 7 deals with the types of fraud that can arise if these checks are not carried out fully. Linked to this is the issue of signing instructions on accounts and liability by individuals for debts that are incurred.

We will then go on to look at the principles of good customer service, as how customers are treated will have a big impact on customer relations. Finally we will take a look at some of the technological innovations that are occurring and how this affects the way that accounts are run.

1.1   There are a number of different types of customers and, therefore, a number of ways that they operate their accounts. This also means that there will be different ways in which the 'banker-customer' relationship operates. An overview of these customers and accounts is as follows:

- *Personal accounts*
  - o   *Sole account – where a customer holds the account in their own name only.*
  - o   *Joint account – where two, or more, customers hold an account together.*
  - o   *Minors – customers who are under the age of 18 generally are unable to enter into contracts, other than to pay for necessities, or contracts that are to their benefit, such as contracts of employment. This means that if financial services providers were to lend to a minor, they would not be able to recover any money should the customer be unable to repay the them. This means that usually minors are not able to arrange overdrafts or loans. An exception might be if they could arrange a parent or guardian to 'guarantee' the loan for them.*
- *Business accounts*
  - o   *Sole traders – a business account where the customer owns their own business.*
  - o   *Partnerships – a group of people running a business together, e.g. a doctors' practice, firms of accountants or solicitors.*
  - o   *Limited companies – again this is a group of persons running a business, however the limited company has a legal entity in its own right – this is known as being 'incorporated', i.e. that they have a certificate to prove that the company exists and is registered as such with Companies House.*
  - o   *Clubs, societies and associations – these can be incorporated or unincorporated.*
  - o   *Executors and trustees – an executor is someone who carries out the instructions left in a person's will and as this usually involves financial transactions, a bank account is required. A trustee is a person who controls assets for a beneficiary and again as this usually involves financial transactions a bank account is required to facilitate this.*

There are various pieces of legislation that affect each of these types of customer account and we will look in more detail at how that legislation affects personal customers.

1.2   Opening customer accounts – this is where the contractual relationship is first established. The account opening procedure follows a number of steps and this is for very good reasons.

The customer offers their funds to the financial services provider for safekeeping and to access the services that the provider offers. As a general rule, the financial services provider accepts these monies. There are of course some exceptions to this rule:

- *If the organisation has previous dealings with this customer and does not wish to deal with them again, perhaps because they incurred bad debts. Another reason for declining an account is that the organisation is unable to identify the customer satisfactorily.*

- *If it becomes apparent that the prospective customer is an undischarged bankrupt. Undischarged bankrupts are limited in the contracts that they can enter into to protect third parties who are unaware of their business failure.*

It is the financial services provider's right to refuse the account if they so wish. This cautiousness at account opening stage is because if the financial services provider was to accept cheques paid into an account that did not belong to the rightful owner, they could be sued for *conversion* by the rightful owner of the funds. If the amounts were large this could result in a substantial loss, not to mention the costs of litigation. There is also the possibility of fraud or money laundering which financial services providers have a duty not to be unwittingly involved in.

The checks to be taken at account opening to ensure that everything is in order are as follows:

- *The customer needs to be able to identify themselves – either by supplying a passport or driving licence and every organisation has their own particular guidelines on this.*

- *The person must be able to prove that they are a fit and proper person to have an account. The financial service provider can usually check this through a Credit Reference Agency search for bad debts and county court judgments. This will provide an indication of how this person conducts their financial affairs, although there are occasions where customers have repaid the debt and it has not been taken off the register. The customer is able to access this information held about them for a small fee directly with the credit reference agency.*

- *The person must be able to prove that they have authority to open the account. This is more in relation to business accounts, an example being where a fraudster obtained company cheques and opens an account in the company name, takes the funds when the cheque has cleared and is never seen again. Again the financial services provider could be sued for conversion and if the amount was large, a loss on the account.*

The account opening form that the customer completes, forms the basis of the contract with their provider and sets out the terms and conditions.

Financial services providers have a number of duties to and rights over their customers once the contractual relationship is entered into:

- *Duty of care as an agent – the provider acts as 'agent' for its customer when it pays or collects a cheque on behalf of a customer and it owes a duty of care. A provider may be liable to a customer if it pays on a forged or altered cheque.*
- *Duty of care as a trustee – the provider owes a duty of care to the beneficiaries of a trust. It is not liable as a trustee unless it has been appointed as one.*
- *Duty of confidentiality – the provider owes its customers an implied duty not to divulge information about them to a third party, it must keep the affairs of its customers secret. However, sometimes the provider will have to divulge information under compulsion of law. This may be in relation to fraud or money laundering offences (see section 4.2).*
- *Banker's opinions – occasionally a bank is asked by another bank, usually on behalf of one of its customers for a reference on one of the account holders. These 'bankers opinion' or 'status enquiries' are little used for personal customers, because of the ease of obtaining information from credit reference agencies. These requests are more commonly used for business customers.*
- *Duty of safe custody – one of the traditional services provided by banks was to hold customers' property in their safekeeping usually in part of the cash safe. Any bank accepting such property has a duty to take care of it. If the bank allowed it to be lost or stolen it could be liable for breach of contract.*
- *Banker's lien – This means that a provider can sell off any securities (stocks and shares) in its possession if a customer has no means to repay an overdraft. This does not include items held in safe custody but it can include government stock, eurobonds and certificates of deposit.*

For joint accounts the following aspects are particularly important for financial services providers as they agree, in accordance with the 'mandate' held, to:

- *Pay, debit or withdraw funds from the account against the signature of either one or more authorised persons.*
- *Deliver any item in safe custody against the written instructions of one or more authorised persons.*

- Make available any balances to the survivor(s) should any one of the account holders die and any items held in safe custody will be available to the survivor(s).
- Treat any liability as unlimited for each account holder.
- Send statements to each account holder unless dispensation is given by the customers to send the statement to one party only.

Facilities that are normally afforded to customers are:

- Chequebooks and plastic cards – customers have a duty of care to safeguard these and must be careful not to encourage any forgery of them.
- Statements.
- Setting up standing orders and direct debits.
- Ordering foreign currency.
- Ability to make payments to third parties by electronic methods (e.g. BACS or CHAPS).

Interestingly, the relationship between the provider and the customer is one of debtor and creditor – not one of trust. There is case law which supports this and the effects are as follows:

- When a customer has deposited money with the provider, the bank becomes the debtor of the customer, i.e. it owes the customer that amount of money. The customer is termed a creditor and the provider will repay the money on demand or after giving an agreed amount of notice. In the meantime the provider can use those funds for any legitimate banking function. The customer cannot restrict the provider in the use of that money.
- The situation is reversed when the customer becomes overdrawn. The customer is now the debtor. The provider has a right of 'set-off' as a result of the debtor/ creditor relationship. This enables the provider to set off a positive balance on one account against a negative balance, where the customer has more than one account. This does not extend to a trust account, so if a parent held a deposit account on behalf of one of their children these funds could not be used to set-off the parent's overdraft.

1.3   The effect of mandates on joint accounts – again this is a very important document and is a legal contract between the financial service provider and its customer. The documentation is usually part of the account opening form, however, if an account is subsequently made joint then customers are usually required to sign a separate form.

Think

What do you think the purpose of a mandate is?

The purpose of a mandate is to establish:

- *Signing instructions on an account where there is more than one party. This can be any one person to sign or all the individuals to sign. If both are to sign, this makes the issue of plastic cards difficult.*
- *Joint and several liability, also known as 'together and each separately'. This means that both parties are equally responsible for any debts incurred on the account.*

A mandate covers instructions for all transactions on the account and most lending arrangements. Failure to complete the mandate correctly at the outset may lead to a number of problems on the account, such as:

- *Embarrassment to the customer when they try to obtain money.*
- *Legal implications for the financial services provider where inaccurate instructions are held, resulting in customer disputes over payments.*
- *Time wasted looking into errors and then correcting them.*

1.4   *Principles of good customer service* – good customer service means different things to different people and there are various groups of people that are responsible for this aspect of the customer relations. It can be very particular to your organisation and even how you think about customer service to what the end result is. There are, however, some basic principles that are common to everyone's view.

Let us look at who are customers are:

Note

Who are your customers?

Customers can be a variety of people, which are divided into two groups:

- *External customers* – these are account holders, individuals who are prospective account holders, third parties you may have to deal with in the course of your work, or even people you met outside work could be classed as customers as they may have some interaction with your organisation in the future.
- *Internal customers* – these are your immediate colleagues in your team, your line manager, staff who you may have responsibility for, other departments and people in other parts of your organisation.

So you can see that every person you come into contact with could be classed as your customer because they rely on you and you rely on them, to get things done.

Note

What do you think customers want?

Generally customers want:

- *Attention* – customers need to feel that they come first, they want to be listened to and to feel that they are being understood.
- *Everyone to be helpful* – whatever your job customer service is always your job.
- *Solutions not problems* – it can be easy to say no, yes is what customers want to hear.
- *A resolution when something goes wrong* – angry customers need to see that you understand them so working out a solution together helps.
- *To feel that they are dealing with a professional person from a trustworthy organisation.*

However, the best way to ascertain what customers want is to ask them. This could be directly asking a customer how they would like a situation resolved to their satisfaction, or seeking how products and services could be improved by way of customer survey questionnaires and focus groups.

Note

What sort of things can you do to ensure excellent customer service?

The individual has a wide variety of things that they can do to provide excellent customer service. These are:

- *Have a genuine interest in customer issues – this can be in both internal or external customer issues.*
- *Display personal empathy, find common ground with the customer.*
- *Create confidence in you and your abilities and what the organisation can do.*
- *Have a consistent approach and be reliable to do what is promised.*
- *A team spirit to work together with colleagues to achieve a common aim.*

The organisation itself has responsibility for ensuring excellent customer service.

Note

What sort of things can the organisation do to ensure excellent customer service?

The organisation can do the following to ensure that customer service is the best it can offer:

- *Offer a quality product and support to customers who use that product.*
- *Ensure that the delivery of that product or service given in a way that satisfies customer needs.*

- *Ensure that the speed of response to phone calls, letters and e-mails is prompt.*
- *Ensure that all staff are trained to handle external customers and their queries.*
- *Put in place monitoring tools to check on each of the above and be able to rectify any shortfalls in service levels.*
- *Offer these products and services at an acceptable price to the customer and at a reasonable profit to the company.*

Note

Why does customer service sometimes go wrong?

Customer service sometimes is not what the customer expects for the following reasons:

- *Pressure of work.*
- *People's personal problems.*
- *Poor management.*
- *Lack of commitment.*
- *An attitude of 'not my job'.*

Colleagues and line managers all have a responsibility to people to help rectify these problems and to ensure that the customer service they provide to all types of customers is the very best they can achieve. The reason for this is that it is very easy to copy a company's products and services, however, it is very difficult to copy the attitude of the staff to the way they deliver customer service. Whilst none of these guidelines is laid down legally, it is the one area where contact centres appear to attract the most criticism. This means that the key role of every member of staff is that they focus on delivering the best possible customer service, as for every customer transaction they deal with, they are representing their organisation.

1.5 Technological innovations in banking (e.g. PC banking, telephone banking) have affected the way that individuals run their accounts in a number of ways. Many customers have started to use these new delivery channels as it suits their lifestyles, being more convenient and accessible than visiting their local branch.

Think

> How do you think this new technology has affected the 'banker/customer relationship'?

There are a number of ways that this new technology has affected the relationship and has provided challenges for the financial service providers. Here are a few of them:

- *Identification at account opening and then subsequently when the account is being run. As with any account it is very important that the customer is identified at the outset. This can then be carried on using passwords or identification numbers as a means of identification. When using websites it is of paramount importance that the site is 'safe', as it would cause an immense scandal if it was found that a site could be entered and account details obtained by unauthorised persons.*
- *Information to make financial decisions must be made available to customers. This may mean sending literature out to customers at regular intervals so they can see what products are available. For websites this information needs to be displayed clearly along with any terms and conditions that are applicable. It is important that any terms and conditions applicable are read by customers, as these form part of the legally binding agreement between the provider and the customer. Often customers will be asked to tick a box to confirm that these have been read.*
- *Problem solving from a distance may become difficult if not handled carefully and therefore systems should be put in place to ensure complaints are resolved effectively and efficiently.*
- *Response times are important as the new technologies speed up the rate of the transaction (think of the speed of e-mail compared to the overland postal service). Customers, therefore, expected an immediate response, even if its just an acknowledgement that their request is being dealt with.*
- *User friendly systems are highly important as is access to an adviser if for some reason, the technology fails.*

You can see that the new technologies present their own challenges that organisations and staff need to overcome, in order to be both legally compliant and also to satisfy their customer's needs.

2.0
Financial Services and Markets Act 2000

2.1   This statute has introduced a new regulatory regime into the financial services sector in the UK and the inception of the Financial Services Authority (FSA), a single regulator. The objectives of the Act are:

- to make provisions for the regulation of financial services markets; and
- to provide for the transfer of statutory functions relating to building societies, industrial, provident societies and certain other mutual societies and for 'connected purposes'.

The FSA is an independent company limited by guarantee and financed through levies on the financial services industry. Her Majesty's Treasury appoints the board, which consists of an Executive Chairman, three managing directors and eleven non-executive directors. This board sets the overall policy but day-to-day decisions and management of the staff are the responsibility of the executive.

Under the Financial Services and Markets Act the FSA has statutory responsibility to:

- Supervise banks under the Banking Act 1987.
- Oversee the regulation of investment business under the Financial Services Act 1986. The Treasury have also contracted with the FSA to undertake most of their functions under insurance legislation.

The statutory objectives of the FSA were dealt with in Unit 2, section 2.0 and the following slide shows how the FSA have interpreted their responsibility in the form of a mission statement:

How do we interpret these objectives? FSA

The New Regulator for the New Millennium summarises the objectives as follows:

"our goal is to maintain efficient, orderly and clean financial markets and help retail consumers achieve a fair deal"

But we do not promise a zero failure regime

Figure 4.1 *How the FSA interprets the statutory objectives laid down by the FSMA 2000, from a FSA presentation 2001.*

Think

> Why is the Regulator unable to offer a 'zero failure' regime?

A zero failure regime would be very difficult to achieve given the large size of the financial services industry, the volume of business it transacts and the dynamic nature of the markets. The resources of the FSA are quite limited compared with the size of the industry. However, given its improved powers and more proactive approach there will be an improvement in the policing of the financial services sector.

The legal framework gives the FSA the power to undertake the following activities:

- *Arrange for the authorisation of firms (organisations) currently operating in insurance, investment and banking businesses.*
- *Arrange for approval of individuals operating in these three areas.*
- *Make rules in the insurance and business sectors.*
- *Gather information and investigate issues.*
- *Intervene, for example to require a firm to stop taking on new business.*
- *To impose financial penalties on authorised firms and approved individuals.*
- *To impose financial penalties on those who abuse investment markets, for example, by insider dealing or market manipulation.*
- *To act as the UK listing authority, taking over this role from the London Stock Exchange.*

The Act is very comprehensive (30 Parts, 425 sections and 22 Schedules) and includes most of the important aspects relating to financial markets and the markets of financial services. By far the biggest impact has been on the regulation of these markets by appointing this new single regulator. The FSMA has replaced a range of regulatory statutes including the Financial Services Act 1986. The FSA has replaced a number of the 'self-regulatory' organisations that oversaw the financial services organisations in the UK. Figure 4.2 shows the organisations whose duties have been absorbed into the FSA.

Figure 4.2 *Organisations whose duties have been absorbed into the FSA.*

2.2   The basis for banking supervision will be looked at in more detail in section 3. We will now look at FSA policy and standards for investment business. The FSA sets standards and/or makes rules where:

- *The importance of a subject as a whole warrants the FSA taking the lead, e.g. on custody of investors assets.*
- *The FSMA requires the FSA to make rules which apply to all investment firms, e.g. on cancellation and the marketing of unregulated collective investment schemes.*

The FSA principles for investment firms (or organisations) are as follows:

- *Integrity – a firm should observe high standards of integrity and fair dealing.*
- *Skill, care and diligence – a firm should act with due skill, care and diligence.*
- *Market practice – a firm should observe high standards of market conduct.*
- *Information about customers – a firm should seek, from its customers, any information about their circumstances and investment objectives which might reasonably be expected to be relevant in enabling it to fulfil its responsibilities to them.*

- *Information for customers* – a firm should take reasonable steps to give a customer it advises, in a comprehensive and timely way, any information needed to enable them to make a balanced and informed decision. A firm should also be ready to provide a customer with a full and fair account of the fulfilment of the responsibilities to them.
- *Conflicts of interest* – a firm should avoid any conflict of interest arising. A firm should not unfairly place its interests above those of its customers.
- *Customer assets* – where a firm has control of customer assets it should arrange proper protection for them by way of segregation and identification of those assets (hence the need for client accounts for customer's money).
- *Financial resources* – a firm should ensure that it maintains adequate financial resources to meet its investment business commitments and to withstand the risks to which its business is subjected.
- *Internal organisation* – a firm should organise and control its internal affairs in a responsible manner, keeping proper records. Where the firm employs staff, or is responsible for the conduct of investment business by others, it should have adequate arrangements to ensure that they are suitably trained and properly supervised and that it has well defined compliance procedures.
- *Relations with regulators* – a firm should deal with it regulator in an open and co-operative manner and keep the regulator promptly informed of anything concerning the firm which might reasonably be expected to be disclosed.

These principles then have to be interpreted by financial services organisations into operational guidelines for staff to follow. One of the most important principles is concerned with investor protection and ensuring that customers receive best advice.

The basis for investor protection was mentioned in Unit 2, section 3.4 under the concept of best advice. Key to this is the concept of 'know your customer' when considering the conduct of investment business. It is an important part of providing investment advice that the provider ensures that the product suggested meets the customer's requirement and that the provider ascertains the knowledge and expertise of the investor. The Financial Services Act 1986 which first highlighted these needs defined four types of investor:

- *Professional investor.*
- *Business investor.*
- *Experienced investor.*
- *Ordinary individual investor.*

The degree of knowledge assumed to be held by each type of investor decreases in the order of the above list. Each person must be assumed to be an ordinary investor unless the person arranging the investment can prove otherwise. This is to ensure that every investor has the correct level of advice for their needs.

There are many details that the investment adviser must gain from the customer. These include the customer's tax position and ability to pay, this is to ensure that the transaction does not place a burden on the customer which could mean that they cannot meet other existing commitments. The adviser must ensure that the customer understands the risks involved, for example, if the customer is investing in unit trusts, that the value of the investment can go down as well as up. Importantly the customer must *understand* these risks, not just have been told them.

There are some exceptions to the 'know your customer' rule:

- *Where the customer is an experienced or professional investor they can be assumed to know the risks involved.*
- *Where the investor is an 'execution only' customer, they are either unwilling to divulge all the relevant information or merely wishes to arrange the investment and not to take any advice about it. Many providers ask the customer to sign a statement to this confirm this type of transaction.*

The customer will enter into an agreement with the provider depending upon the type of transaction they are entering into. Where a provider is giving investment advice it must give the best advice possible. The provider must record all the facts that have led to this advice, bearing in mind all the customer personal circumstances, such as tax position, disposable income, assets, etc. Also, the provider must give warnings about any possible dangers and associated risks. It is important the product is suitable for the customer's needs.

If the customer is not likely to benefit from the type of investments on offer then no sale should be made. If the transaction is 'execution only' then the best advice regulations do not apply.

2.3   There are some serious implications for contact centre staff not observing the FSMA rules. People (approved persons) who are likely to require approval from the FSA are:

- *An individual selling designated products.*
- *A research analyst.*
- *A corporate financier.*
- *A fund manager.*
- *An investment adviser.*
- *A senior compliance officer.*
- *A money laundering reporting officer.*
- *A director or senior manager.*

The only exceptions to the requirements are those people who deal with current accounts, deposits and general insurance. However, these individuals should not be taking on any responsibilities of the approved persons listed above. This means they should not get into any dialogue with customers about their investment needs, be seen to be giving advice or making recommendations about investment products.

There is an increased emphasis on staff having individual responsibility with a greater onus on senior managers being responsible and accountable for their actions of their staff. It also means that, for the first time, some back office staff will have to be approved and may have to take new examinations in order to satisfy the new regulations.

To become and remain an approved person you must be deemed 'fit and proper' in accordance with a number of factors specified by the FSA. These relate to:

- *Honesty.*
- *Integrity and reputation.*
- *Competence and capability.*
- *Financial soundness.*

The FSA requires organisations to provide training designed to ensure that employees are competent and continue to be so. It has the power to withdraw approval if it considers that a person is not longer 'fit and proper' to perform the controlled function to which approval relates. As an approved person you also have a personal obligation to ensure you remain competent of carrying out your role. Many organisations will only allow their advisers a set number of attempts at undertaking regulatory exams such as Certificate for Financial Advisors (CeFA) or Certificate in Mortgage Advice and Practice (CeMAP). This is because the qualifications are a requirement for these individuals to undertake their roles.

Approved people are subject to a wide range of regulatory requirements and have to comply with a set of principles. They are issued with a code of practice – consisting of rules and guidelines – applying to the business that they undertake for their business. Much of this information is set out in the FSA Handbook of Rules and Guidance.

2.4 *Insider dealing and market abuse* – insider dealing broadly covers situations where a person buys or sells securities when he, but not the other party to the transaction, is in possession of confidential information which affects the value to be placed on those securities. Insider dealing has been a criminal offence since 1976 but very few prosecutions have been brought and still fewer convictions obtained. This is despite the commonly-held perception that insider dealing does occur, in particular in the shares of companies which shortly afterwards become the target of a takeover. The new offence of 'market abuse' was created in the FSMA in order to improve enforcement.

Much of the legislation is connected with stock market transactions in terms of 'market manipulation' and 'misuse of privileged information', however, it is important for all individuals working within a financial services environment to understand that the rules exist and at some point they could inadvertently become subject to the rulings. An example could be whereby you knew that a new product or service was going to be launched that could have a positive affect on the share price of your employer's company. Using this knowledge to encourage people to buy shares for a profit could be deemed 'misuse of privileged information'.

Insider dealing is currently defined by the Criminal Justice Act 1993 which makes it an offence for a person who has confidential, price-sensitive information relating to securities to deal in those securities or encourage others to do so. Note that no offence takes place if a person encourages another not to deal, e.g. not to sell shares in a company about to be taken over that he was about to sell. It is also an offence for a person to disclose confidential, price-sensitive information, other than in the bona fide course of his employment. The confidential information in question will generally be in his possession because of some connection which he has with the company whose securities are to be dealt with (e.g. he may be a director, employee or professional advisor of that company), or because someone in such a position has provided him, directly or indirectly, with the information.

An individual has information as an insider, if the information is inside information, he knows it to be inside information and he knows that he has that information from an inside source. There is no requirement to show a connection between the individual insider and the issuer of the securities.

There are a number of defences available to a person charged with insider dealing. These are that:

- *He did not at the time expect the dealing to result in a profit attributable to the fact that the information in question was price-sensitive information in relation to the securities.*
- *At the time he believed, on reasonable grounds, that the information had been disclosed widely enough to ensure that none of those taking part in the dealing would be prejudiced by not having the information.*
- *He would have done what he did even if he had not had the information.*

Defences to the offence of encouraging another to deal are that:

- *He did not at the time expect the dealing to result in a profit attributable to the fact that the information in question was price-sensitive information in relation to the securities.*

- *At the time he believed on reasonable grounds that the information had been disclosed widely enough to ensure that none of those taking part in the dealing would be prejudiced by not having the information.*
- *He would have done what he did even if he had not had the information.*

Defences to the offence of disclosing confidential information are that:

- *He did not at the time expect any person, because of the disclosure, to deal in securities.*
- *Although he had such an expectation at the time, he did not expect the dealing to result in a profit attributable to the fact that the information was price-sensitive information in relation to the securities.*

Given the way the offence is drafted, and the defences to it, it is easy to understand why there have been so few convictions for insider dealing offences.

Market abuse is described as a civil offence. It is not a crime but the FSA will have the power to impose a penalty on offenders. Market abuse is defined as behaviour in relation to qualifying investments on relevant markets, which is likely to be regarded by a regular user of that market as a failure to observe the standard of behaviour reasonably expected of a person in that position in the market. In order to be an offence, the behaviour must also fulfil one of three criteria:

- *It is based on information which is not generally available but which, if available, a regular user of the market would regard as relevant to deciding the terms on which transactions in that investment should be effected.*
- *It is likely to give a regular user of the market a false or misleading impression of the supply or demand, or price or value of that investment.*
- *A regular user of that market would consider it likely to distort the market in that investment.*

The FSMA requires the FSA to produce a Code of Conduct on Market Abuse. This Code offers guidance on what constitutes market abuse. The FSA can enforce the regime through court injunctions or a hearing through its own administrative process, the Regulatory Decisions Committee (RDC).

The RDC is a body to set up to take all enforcement decisions. It is separate from the FSA's investigative staff. The RDC will decide on the level of financial penalties to be imposed, restitution and compensation and the relationship between civil offences and criminal proceedings.

3.0
The basis for banking supervision

As shown above, the FSA has taken over the supervisory functions of the Bank of England. Central to this system will be the threshold conditions in the FSMA, and the FSA Handbook. The FSA will be the sole supervisory body for banks and for insurance companies and building societies.

The Banking Act 1987 is the current source of supervision law. It prohibits anyone from accepting a deposit in the course of carrying on a deposit-taking business unless they are an authorised institution. Non-authorised institutions are also prohibited from using any name that indicates they carry on a banking business, or otherwise holding themselves out as a bank. Authorised institutions include both those institutions authorised by the UK authorities and also those authorised by their European Economic Area (EEA) home countries. This is the notion of the European 'single passport' for financial institutions. Once authorised in their home state, they are able, without further authorisation, to do business anywhere in the EEA. The FSA holds the residual power to prohibit deposit-taking by an EEA institution in certain circumstances. UK banks are able to do business in other EEA states on a similar basis.

Institutions, which wish to seek authorisation from the FSA, currently must satisfy the regulator on all of the relevant criteria:

- *The directors, controllers and managers are fit and proper persons for the positions they hold.*
- *A minimum of two people effectively direct the business.*
- *There are sufficient non-executive directors.*
- *The business is conducted in a prudent manner.*
- *The institution maintains its own funds and other resources sufficient to safeguard the interests of depositors, adequate liquidity and adequate provision for depreciation in the value of its assets.*
- *The institution has initial capital of at least five million euros.*
- *The business will be carried out with integrity and appropriate professional skills.*

Even after authorisation has been granted, the FSA has the power to revoke authorisation or to restrict authorisation at any time. Banks can appeal against a refusal, a revocation, or a restriction of authorisation.

Banks authorised by the UK supervisor must notify the FSA about changes of directors, controllers or managers. They must also notify of significant shareholders (someone who acquires 5% of the bank's voting power). Large exposures (10% of available capital) must also be notified. The FSA has power to require banks to provide information and documents. Providing false or misleading information is a criminal offence. The FSA also has power to appoint an investigator to look into a bank, and obstructing an investigation is a criminal offence.

Banks must keep audited accounts available for inspection by the FSA. They must also inform the FSA of any proposal to change its auditors. Following the lessons learned from the closure of BCCI, auditors now have a legal duty to tell the FSA of any matters that give them reasonable cause to believe the bank no longer fulfils the minimum criteria for authorisation. The FSA has the power to petition the court to wind up a bank on grounds that it is unable to pay its debts or that it is just and equitable so to do. The FSA Guide to Banking Supervision contains extensive information on prudential supervision and capital adequacy.

To obtain authorisation an application must be made to the FSA including a statement setting out the nature and scale of the proposed business together with its management arrangements. There must be a minimum criteria met to gain authorisation showing that the organisation is capable of providing:

- *current or deposit account facilities in sterling or foreign currency to members of the public and corporate bodies;*
- *finance in the form of loans and overdrafts;*
- *foreign exchange facilities for domestic and foreign customers;*
- *finance though bills of exchange and promissory notes;*
- *finance for foreign trade and documentation in connection with foreign trade;*
- *financial advice for the general public and corporate bodies;*
- *investment management services; and*
- *arranging the purchase or sale of securities.*

These stringent rules means that members of the public are not misled and are opening accounts and obtaining services from reputable organisations.

3.1   The Banking Code

Think

What is the Banking Code?

The Banking Code is a voluntary code of practice drawn up by the British Bankers Association, the Building Societies Association and the Association for Payment Clearing Services in 1992 to set standards of good practice which should be followed as a minimum. It has been revised four times, most lately in 2000. It is to be observed by banks, building societies and card issuers in their dealings with personal customers. A personal customer, in this instance, is defined as a private individual who holds an account or uses services offered by that financial services provider. The account can be a joint account with another private individual, or the customer as an executor or a trustee may hold it. **You should obtain a copy of the Code as it is very important in customer facing roles.**

Compliance to the Code is handled by the Banking Code Standards Board (BCSB).

The Code has 11 key comments. In this financial services providers will:

(1) *Act fairly and reasonably.*
(2) *Ensure that all services and products comply with the Code, even if they have their own terms and conditions.*
(3) *Give information on services and products in plain language and offer help if there is any aspect which the customer does not understand.*
(4) *Help customers to choose a product or service to fit their needs.*
(5) *help customers to understand the financial implications of:*
   o   *a mortgage;*
   o   *other borrowing;*
   o   *savings and investment products; and*
   o   *card products.*
(6) *Help customers understand how their account works.*
(7) *Have safe, secure and reliable banking and payment systems.*
(8) *Ensure that the procedures staff follow reflect these commitments.*
(9) *Correct errors and handle complaints speedily.*
(10) *Consider cases of financial difficulty and mortgage arrears sympathetically and positively.*
(11) *Ensure that all services and products comply with relevant laws and regulations.*

Financial services providers must also comply with relevant legislation, judicial decisions and other codes of conduct applicable to their businesses.

Customers must be provided with relevant information in writing about products and services including charges and rates of interest, operation of accounts, lending criteria and the rules regarding credit facilities. This information is usually provided when the account is opened but should also be available upon request.

Confidentiality of customer information – under the Code financial services providers are required to treat all customer details in the strictest confidence and not to disclose information to a third party without the customer's consent, unless there is a overriding legal requirement to do so.

The four situations in which disclosure is permitted are:

• *If the customer requests or consents to disclosure.*
• *If the financial services provider is legally compelled to do so, examples being in connection with drug-trafficking and the prevention of terrorism.*

- *If it is in the financial service provider's interests to disclose, for instance if the customer has defaulted on loan repayments, the customer is given 28 days' notice before the default is registered with a credit reference agency.*
- *If there is a duty to the public to disclose, for example, if a customer is trading with an enemy at a time of war.*

Employees must take care not to disclose customer information inadvertently. They should not talk about customers' accounts among themselves, outside work, or to their friends or relatives. This also extends to taking documentation about customers off the premises and taking care to dispose of customer documentation in the correct way.

There are some other aspects of the code, which are important:

- *Marketing of services – financial service providers cannot justify disclosing customer details to a third party for marketing purposes by claiming that it is in the organisation's best interest. They must have the customer's written consent to pass the customer's name to a third party within a marketing group. Organisations are also not allowed to make the provision of a service, such as opening a bank account, conditional of giving this consent.*

  When the customer opens an account, the financial services provider must give the customer the chance to say he does not want to receive marketing literature.

  When a financial services provider advertises its lending services it must make clear that applications for loans will be subject to appraisal of the customer's financial standing. The advertising and promotional literature must be fair and reasonable with no misleading information.

- *Handling customer complaints – under the Code financial services providers must establish internal procedures for handling customer complaints in a fair and timely manner and inform customers of these procedures. Staff dealing directly with customers must also be aware of how to handle these complaints. Financial services providers must belong to one of the authorised Ombudsman or Arbitration schemes such as the Banking Ombudsman/Building Societies Ombudsman which is now overseen by the FSA (see 3.2).*

- *There are a large number of other aspects of the code which contain guidelines. The ones which have been updated most recently include:*
  - *Financial providers offering a basic account will be required to tell customers about the account. These basic accounts are being developed by banks to promote financial inclusion and as such need to be explained fully.*
  - *Ash machine charges – a message on the screen will warn customers before they commit to the transaction of the amount of any charge for the transaction and will tell them who is making the charge. No customer will be double-charged for a cash withdrawal from an ATM.*

- o *Branch closures – financial services providers planning to close branches will be required to give eight weeks' notice and to advise customers of alternative arrangements.*
- o *Helping customers to choose – for all retail banking products financial service providers will be obliged to give customers information on which they can make informed choices about products to fit their needs.*
- o *How to deal with customers who are experiencing financial difficulties and advise them where they can get free advice.*
- o *New distribution channels – the revised code applies to all banking services to personal customers irrespective of whether they are provided through branches, by the Internet, by phone or by any other means.*

Think

What is the effect of the Banking Code on your role?

The effect of the Banking Code on the day-to-day role of staff is far reaching. Here are some of the implications you may well have come up with:

- *Always ensure that you can positively identify your customer if the telephone system hasn't already done this for you. Giving customer details to unauthorised persons is in direct contravention of the Code.*
- *Ensure that customers receive full details of any products that they are thinking about using, whether that is directly from you during a call or via product literature that is sent out to them.*
- *If part of your role is to deal with customer complaints, ensure that you know how the complaints procedure works and what a customer can do if they are still not satisfied (see section 3.2). Ensure that you deal with the complaint promptly or if you can't pass it to someone who can.*
- *Don't use jargon when dealing with customers – remember information on financial services must be in plain language.*
- *Ensure that you know how the products and services work so that if you need to you can explain these fully to the customer.*

3.2   Making complaints – in recent times there has been a sharp increase in complaints from the public regarding financial services. The advent of TESSAs and endowment mortgages, for example, has seen a 30 per cent rise in the number of cases ombudsmen have been asked to investigate.

The Financial Service Ombudsman Service (FOS), created by the FSMA 2000, will be launched in April 2002 and will create a single independent body to adjudicate on all complaints from members of the public and small businesses. The following eight separate ombudsmen will be gathered up into one department:

- *The Personal Investment Authority (PIA) Ombudsman.*
- *The Investment Ombudsman.*
- *The Securities and Futures Authority (SFA) Complaints Bureau and Arbitration Service.*
- *The Financial Services Authority (FSA) Complaints Unit.*
- *The Banking Ombudsman.*
- *The Building Societies Ombudsman.*
- *The Insurance Ombudsman (IOB).*
- *The Personal Insurance Arbitration Service (PIAS).*

These bodies have already been brought together under one roof pending the change of name. The rules have been standardised combining best practice across banking and loans, insurance and investment, each of which has its own principal ombudsman with a team reporting to them.

The following three bodies will remain outside the scope of the FSA for the time being:

- *The Pensions Advisory Service (OPAS) – provides initial advice and conciliation for complaints about employers' pension schemes and personal pension providers.*
- *The Pensions Ombudsman – for employers' pension schemes and personal pension providers. Formally decides on complaints not sorted out by OPAS.*
- *The Mortgage Code Arbitration Scheme – mortgage intermediaries and some mortgage lenders (e.g. brokers, estate agents, financial advisers and mortgage lenders which are not banks or building societies).*

A principal change is that under the FOS that membership of the service will no longer be discretionary. It is a statutory scheme, which covers financial service providers, regardless of their wish to be covered. There is a maximum compensation limit of £100,000.

The EU E-Commerce Directive will affect the FOS. This declares that regulation; compensation and redress in relation to e-Commerce should be dealt with where the business is based. So where a UK bank offers Internet banking with other countries, complaints arising from these customers should be dealt with in the UK under the FOS. If a UK resident uses an Internet bank offered by a non-UK provider they will not be able to use the FOS but will have to use a local scheme, if one exists. This is a good point to raise with customers if they mention they are thinking about transferring their account to a foreign provider.

Another major change is that, for the first time, banks will have to publish figures on their customer service. They must collate statistics on the number of complaints received from personal customers and small businesses and submit a twice-yearly report to the FSA. Included in the report will be the type of complaint it relates to, for example, administrative error or charges.

The FSMA made it a statutory requirement that a complaint must receive a final response within eight weeks of the first date of the complaint. If not resolved the complaint can be referred to the ombudsman within six months.

So how should a customer go about making a complaint and how should it be dealt with? All organisations have a procedure for to follow, however, this is an example of best practice showing how a complaint can be escalated and hopefully resolved:

- *A customer tells you that they are not happy with the product or service. Try to resolve the complaint immediately and take ownership of the complaint, even if it wasn't personally your fault.*
- *The complaint cannot be resolved immediately so you:*
  - *advise the customer of the action you will take to investigate the complaint; then*
  - *provide the customer with a contact name and telephone number for the person who is looking after the complaint;*
  - *provide the customer with a written acknowledgement of the complaint; and*
  - *keep the customer advised of progress at all times.*
- *If the customer is still not happy with the outcome of this investigation then they are within their rights to take the complaint higher within the company. In the absence of a proper complaints procedure they can write to the most senior person in the organisation. Customers should be encouraged to keep copies of any letters and paperwork relating to their complaint as it may be useful further along in the process.*
- *If they reach a situation of 'deadlock' and the organisation writes to the complainant stating that they have reached this position, then they can have the matter referred to an independent ombudsman, assuming that there is an ombudsman that oversees the type of complaint they are making. The organisation's documentation and paperwork should state which body regulates them and therefore which is the relevant independent complaints scheme. The ombudsman is able to make decisions that bind an organisation to compensate the customer. Any compensation given will relate to actual loss they have incurred.*
- *If needs be the complaint can then be resolved through the courts, or by 'arbitration' which is a cheaper alternative to legal proceedings. However, customers are advised that if an Ombudsman has not found in their favour then it is unlikely that a court would overturn that judgment.*

Here some examples of complaints that have been brought against financial service providers:

- *After taking financial advice Mr A invested a large sum of money in a unit trust investing a UK companies. Its performance was poor despite a big rise in the stock market. Mr A complained that the unit trust's fund managers were incompetent. Mr A's complaint was turned down because if he took financial advice and, as long as the nature of the investment and the associated risks, were adequately explained to Mr A in the beginning, poor investment performance is not normally grounds for upholding a complaint.*
- *A customer paid for goods from Ms B's business. After checking with their bank that the customer's cheque for £550 had cleared, Ms B released the goods. The next day she found that the cheque had bounced. Ms B complained to the bank but neither party could agree the outcome. Ms B decided to take the case to the independent ombudsman. The ombudsman ruled that the bank should refund Ms B because the bank had not adequately explained to her what the term 'cleared' meant. The ombudsman noted that many people do not understand the clearing system and the term 'cleared' is often misunderstood. It means simply that evidence of a deposit has reached the customer's account and you are allowed to withdraw funds against it, it is not a guarantee that the cheque will not bounce.*
- *Mr C claimed he was advised to take out a personal pension plan. Two years earlier, he had taken his own decision to opt out of his employer's pension scheme. Despite the adviser encouraging him to rejoin his employer's scheme Mr C took out the personal pension plan instead. Mr C complained that the adviser had given him bad advice. The firm the adviser worked for did not agree. There was strong evidence on Mr C's file that he had been determined to follow his own advice.*

These examples illustrate the potential minefield that members of staff can find themselves. This is why approved advisers have to carry out their fact finds very thoroughly and record all the details. It is also important for those members of staff who carry out day-to-day activities do so correctly, as the example about the cheque clearing shows.

Whilst the procedure is in place for customers, it is obviously better not to get into this type of situation in the first place. To minimise the risk of complaints, customers should be encouraged to:

- *Read all information they are given, especially the small print.*
- *Ask questions about anything they don't understand.*
- *Check any information about the benefits of an investment or the rate at which their investment will grow. These benefits are usually just an illustration not a guarantee of what they will get back in the future.*
- *Make sure they understand the nature of any risks involved.*

- Make sure they understand any charges, especially if there is any danger of them not being able to keep up the payments.

If customers think they have a complaint and are not sure how to make it they can either contact the FSA Consumer Helpline or their local Citizens Advice Bureau for further assistance.

3.3 *Compensation schemes* – the FSA has launched a new single Financial Services Compensation Scheme (FSCS) that replaced the eight existing arrangements through the following bodies:

- The Deposit Protection Scheme.
- The Building Society Investor Protection Scheme.
- The Policy Holders Protection Scheme.
- The Friendly Societies Protection Scheme.
- The Investors Compensation Scheme.
- The Section 43 Scheme.
- The Personal Investment Authority Indemnity Scheme.
- The arrangement between the Association of British Insurers and the Investor Compensation Scheme Ltd for paying compensation to widows, widowers and dependents of deceased persons.

The FSCS provides compensation if an organisation collapses owing money to investors, depositors or policyholders. The compensation is a final 'safety net' for consumers when a financial services provider goes out of business and it provides a key part of the FSA framework to provide appropriate protection for consumers. Consumers will benefit from having a one point of contact for queries and claims rather than having to chose one from an array of different bodies.

In setting up the new scheme the FSA is seeking to provide a reasonable level of compensation to individual customers and small business that have lost money through the collapse of a bank, building society, insurer or investment firm.

The compensation limits for the scheme are as follows:

- Deposits – £31,700 (100% of £2,000 and 90% of £33,000).
- Investments – £48,000 (100% of £30,000 and 90% of next £20,000).
- Long-term insurance at least 90% of the value of the policyholder's guaranteed fund at the date of default.
- General insurance – compulsory, 100% of valid claim/unexpired premiums; non-compulsory, 100% of the first £2,000 of valid claim/unexpired premiums and 90% of the remainder of the claim.

The FSCS is funded by levies on the industry on a pay-as-you-go basis to be able to support this scheme. This gives customers the peace of mind that they will have some right of recourse should the unthinkable happen.

3.4   *The Human Rights Act 1998* – The Human Rights Act enacts into UK law the European Convention on Human Rights. Despite the title of the Convention, corporations as well as individuals are protected by it. One of the rights in the Convention is the right to a fair trial (Article 6). An independent and impartial tribunal must conduct all civil and criminal trials. The trial must take place within a reasonable period and there is a right to a public hearing. Defendants in criminal trials additionally have the right to the presumption of innocence, the right to protection from self-incrimination, the right to examine witnesses and the right to receive full disclosure of the nature of the accusation against them. There is a considerable body of case law in European courts dealing with the interpretation of the Convention. This case law defines matters such as what constitutes a criminal trial.

The Convention may have an impact on a number of areas in the law of financial services. The most obvious application is in the area of financial services regulation. Wherever an institution can be prosecuted or penalised for an infringement of the regulations, there is scope for a claim by that institution that its rights under the Convention were not respected by the process that was adopted. This is all the more likely when a tribunal other than a court imposed the prosecution or penalty. Examples of susceptible areas include the new civil offence of market abuse, and the powers of the statutory Financial Ombudsman Scheme.

Market abuse is described as a civil offence in the FSMA but under the Convention it may be considered criminal, providing defendants with all the commensurate additional rights under the Convention. The Convention does not specifically define the appropriate standard of proof in criminal trials, but the market abuse standard of the balance of probabilities may be considered a breach of the defendant's rights if market abuse is considered a criminal offence under the Convention.

The Financial Ombudsman Service (FOS) operates as a tribunal resolving civil disputes. The FOS rules discriminate in favour of complainants in some ways, e.g. it will be a compulsory scheme for banks whilst it is voluntary for customers who can go to court if they prefer, and banks are bound by decisions of the FOS whereas customers can ignore them. It may be that the Convention will consider these rules deny banks' right to a fair trial.

Additionally, the FOS is able to reach a decision based on non-legal grounds, e.g. on the basis of what is considered fair and it can increase the level of awards on the same basis. It has been suggested that this may be in breach of the bank's right to peaceful enjoyment of possessions or be contrary to the prohibition on the arbitrary deprivation of property.

Finally, it is possible that customers of banks may invoke the Convention. In

Lloyds Bank v Dix, the claimant bank sought possession of a property following default by the mortgagors. At the court hearing, the defendants asked for an adjournment because they had no legal representative present. The trial judge refused to adjourn the case and, after hearing the case, granted the bank possession. The defendants appealed on the basis that their right to a fair trial under Article 6 had been breached. The Court of Appeal held that there was no requirement to send a case back for re-trial where the defendant's case was patently hopeless.

4.0
The Mortgage Code

This section looks at the Mortgage Code and what this means for the customer in terms of service they receive and what level of compensation is available to them.

The Mortgage Code is concerned with providing important protection for customers when they take out a mortgage. The Code sets out:

- *How the customer's mortgage should be arranged.*
- *What information the customer should receive before they commit themselves.*
- *How the customer's mortgage should be dealt with once it is in place.*

If a lender (or intermediary) fails to meet the standards of the Code and the customer suffers as a result, then the customer has the right to compensation under a compulsory independent complaints scheme.

Choosing a mortgage

There are three different levels of service that the mortgage lender (or intermediary) may provide to help the customer choose a suitable mortgage. The lender is obliged to tell the customer at the beginning of the process which of these levels of service they can provide. These levels are:

- *Advice and a recommendation on which of the mortgages the lender can provide for the customer is the most suitable for them.*
- *Information on the different types of mortgage product on offer so that the customer can make an informed decision of the choice they wish to make.*
- *Information on a single mortgage product only if only one mortgage is available or if the customer has already made up their mind.*

The customer should check that they understand which level of service is being offered and what it means for them. Whichever level of service is provided, the lender (or intermediary) should give the customer the information on all the following areas of the mortgage:

- *The repayment method (e.g. interest only or capital and interest) and the repayment period.*
- *The financial consequences of repaying the mortgage early.*
- *The type of interest rate – variable, fixed, discounted, capped and so on.*
- *What the future repayments will be after any fixed or discounted period.*
- *Whether the customer is required to take any insurance services with the mortgage and if so whether the insurance must be arranged by the lender (or intermediary).*
- *The costs and fees that might be involved with the mortgage – valuation fees, arrangement fees, legal fees and early redemption fees.*
- *Whether the customer can continue with their chosen mortgage if they wish to move house.*
- *When the customer's account details may be passed to credit reference agencies.*
- *Whether the customer needs to pay a high percentage lending fee and if so, what this means for the customer.*

If the customer is using the services of an intermediary to arrange the loan they must tell the customer if they are receiving a fee from the lender for introducing the mortgage to the lender. They must also let the customer know whether they usually arrange mortgages from a number of selected lenders or from the market place as a whole.

Before the mortgage is completed the lender (or intermediary) must confirm in writing the level of service they have provided and the reasons for any mortgage recommendation (if a recommendation has been given). The customer should ensure that they fully understand this written confirmation and be provided guidance if they do not.

The Code's main commitments

The Code has ten main commitments. Broadly these are that lenders and intermediaries will:

- *act fairly and reasonably with the customer at all times;*
- *make sure that all services and products keep to the conditions of the Code, even if the financial services providers have their own terms and conditions;*
- *give customers information on products and services in plain language and offer help if there is any area which the customer does not understand;*
- *help the customer to choose a mortgage to fit their needs unless they have already decided on a mortgage;*

- *help the customer understand the financial effects of a mortgage;*
- *help the customer understand how a mortgage account works;*
- *make sure that the procedures that staff follow reflect the commitment set out in the code;*
- *correct errors and handle complaints speedily;*
- *consider cases of financial difficulty and mortgage arrears sympathetically and positively;*
- *make sure that all products and services meet the relevant laws and regulations.*

How mortgage lenders and intermediaries keep to the Mortgage Code is monitored independently by the Mortgage Board or is authorised through the FSA. Any organisation under the Code will be a member of a recognised complaints scheme, which gives the customer an extra level of protection as these schemes award compensation of up to £100,000 if the customer should suffer as a result of their lender or intermediary failing to keep to the code. The complaints process is similar to that of the Financial Services Ombudsman as a series of escalatory exchanges resulting in referral to the Mortgage Code Arbitration Scheme if deadlock occurs. Mortgages are becoming subject to more stringent regulation and, unless you are an approved person, you *should not* enter into detailed discussions with a customer about their mortgage requirements.

5.0
The Consumer Credit Act 1974

This section looks at the Consumer Credit Act 1974 and how it applies to the role of the contact centre staff involved in lending.

The purpose of the Consumer Credit Act 1974 (CCA) is to regulate, supervise and control certain types of lending to individuals and to provide borrowers with protection from unscrupulous lenders. The provisions of the CCA are regulated by the Office of Fair Trading (OFT) and backed by certain European Union powers. As the Act came into force some time ago it will be subject to a review and it is likely that some revisions to it will be made in the future.

There are many types of lender in the financial services market, ranging from large multi-national banks to individual moneylenders. The CCA sets out standards by which all lenders must conduct their business. It includes a number of safeguards by which potential borrowers are made aware of the nature and conditions of a loan.

5.1 The CCA affects most aspects of lending activities by financial services providers, including personal loans and revolving credit such as credit cards. Not all loans are covered by the Act:

- Loans up to £25,000 are regulated by the CCA, those in excess of this figure are exempt from the provisions of the Act.
- Loans for the purchase, improvement or repair of private dwellings are exempt. Loans which are backed by a legal charge over a dwelling, but used for other purposes, are not exempt.

5.2 The main elements of the Consumer Credit Act's provisions are:

- The providers of the loans that are regulated by the Act must be licensed by the OFT.
- Prospective borrowers have a 'cooling-off' period during which they can review the terms of their loan and, if they wish, can decide not to proceed with the trans-action. This clause was inserted in to the CCA to prevent salespeople entering people's houses and charging excessive amounts in credit agreements. This does not apply if:
  o the arrangement was made over the telephone; or
  o the credit agreement was signed on the premises of the person or organisation who provided or arranged the credit.
- Customers must be given a written copy of the credit agreement, which will show the cash price, the total charge for credit and the Annual Percentage Rate or APR. One of the Act's most significant innovations was this new system for comparing the cost of borrowing. Every regulated loan must quote the APR so that borrowers can evaluate the cost of borrowing with that of other lenders. The APR allows for the rate of interest and also other charges associated with the loan, such as setting up fees. This usually means that the APR will be higher than the contractual interest rate being charged for the loan. In July 2001 the OFT sent letters to 40 financial service providers demanding that they make immediate changes to the way they advertised their APR as it was misleading to customers. They were warned that if they failed to do so the OFT would issue 'stop now' orders. This shows that the OFT has the power to take drastic action on behalf of consumers if it needs to.
- There is one very significant provision of the Act. Where a seller of goods and ser-vices grants a customer credit, or arranges for the customer to obtain credit from a third party, if the customer has a claim against a seller (e.g. in the event of failure to supply the goods or the supply of faulty goods) and has paid for them by an agreement regulated by the Act, the seller of the goods and the provider of the credit are jointly liable. This means that customers can claim compensation from the credit provider should they wish to. The rule applies to purchases valued between £100 and £30,000 and also applies to credit card purchases. It is esti-mated that credit card companies in the UK pay out £20 million per year as a result of such claims from cardholders.

- A lender cannot demand early repayment, try to get the goods back or end the agreement without first serving a written notice on the customer. This has to give the customers seven days' notice and is called a 'default notice'. The notice has to be written in a particular way and should contain the following:
  - How much should be paid to bring the payments up-to-date.
  - When payments should be made.
  - How the agreement can be brought to an end and that if payments are made the agreement will not be brought to an end.
- The customer has the right to repay the loan at any time, in full and it should be possible for them to do so.

Is important for financial services staff with responsibility for lending to:

- Follow the strict procedures as set out by the CCA 1974 and subsequent regulations. The correct forms must be used and the correct information must be completed as this is because the documentation forms an agreement between the provider and the customer and all the relevant details should be made available to customers. A court has already observed that the automatic unenforceability of a loan agreement resulting from a 'misstatement of the prescribed terms' may constitute a breach of the lender's rights under Article 6 of the Human Rights Act.
- The customer can ask for a written quotation and the lender is obliged to do so. The regulations specify what must be included in this quotation. This is to ensure that prospective borrowers are able to obtain the necessary information to consider what loan suits them best before committing themselves.
- Make sure the forms are posted promptly to the customer and that copies are received that have been signed by the customer.
- Ensure that default procedures are followed correctly – these could be the cause of complaint by a customer if not followed and that dates for sending out default notices are adhered to.
- Any amendments to a customer's account information are made in line with the agreement forms as incorrect limits and interest rates could lead to complaints later.

6.0
Money laundering

This section deals with money laundering regulations and the duty of care on contact centre staff to report any suspicious transactions.

Money laundering is the process by which money obtained illegally is made to appear as if it had been obtained legally. The nature, source and ownership of those criminal proceeds are concealed by a large variety of methods. The consequence is that the origins of entitlement to the money are disguised and the money can again be used to the benefit of a criminal and/or their associates.

The criminal activity from which the proceeds are derived can be of any kind, ranging from tax evasion to drug trafficking. The methods used to disguise the origin and/or ownership of these proceeds are infinite and various. Essentially the money launderer has two weapons – secrecy, and ease with which money can be transferred within the international financial markets.

- *If the money launderer is able to deposit illicit proceeds within an institution or place that required little or no disclosure concerning the ownership of those funds, it may be difficult to trace the property back to its criminal source.*
- *If money is passed though a complicated series of transactions (known as layering), involving legitimate as well as illegitimate enterprises, it may again be impossible to identify the owner of that money.*

If the ownership of the funds cannot be ascertained, it is virtually impossible to establish that they are the product of criminal activity. The funds can then be reused in legitimate activity. This reuse of the funds is known as *integration*.

6.1   The legal definitions of the crime of money laundering are as follows:

- *The conversion or transfer of property for the purpose of concealing or disguising the origin of the property.*
- *The concealment or disguise of the true nature, source, location, disposition, movement, rights to or ownership of illicitly gained property.*
- *The acquisition, possession or use of property derived from criminal activity or participation in criminal activity.*

These are the definitions employed in the European Union Council Directive of 1991. They have in the main been adopted in subsequent UK legislation. The Directive also provides that all European Union member states should ensure that all financial and credit institutions located within the national member states should implement certain internal procedures and controls. The aim of those controls is as follows:

- **Deterrence**: *to prevent credit and financial institutions being used for money laundering purposes.*
- **Co-operation**: *to ensure that there is co-operation between credit and financial institutions and law enforcement agencies.*
- **Detection**: *to establish customer identification and record keeping procedures within all financial and credit institutions which will assist the law enforcement agencies in detecting, tracing and prosecuting money launderers.*

The Directive envisages that these provisions will enable the financial sector to play a powerful role in combating money laundering and consequently criminal activity.

Additionally, it foresees that regulation of this kind will maintain public confidence in the soundness and stability of the European financial system.

The Criminal Justice Act 1993 and the Money Laundering Regulations 1993 were enacted in order to implement the European Council Directive of 1991 on money laundering.

6.2   The regulations now provide that failure by a financial services provider to implement and maintain the internal systems and training required by the regulations will result in criminal liability on the part of the financial institution's directors, managers, partners or officers.

- **Individual liability** – *the legislation in relation to individual liability is contained in different laws depending upon the source of the criminal proceeds, whether the money to be laundered results from terrorist activities, drug trafficking or other criminal conduct.*

   In essence, however, it is an offence for an individual to commit any of the following types of actions:
   - *To assist another person to launder proceeds obtained from drug trafficking or other criminal conduct or terrorist funds.*
   - *To fail to report knowledge or suspicions of the laundering of drug trafficking proceeds or terrorist funds.*
   - *To provide information to another person which is likely to prejudice an investigation into drug trafficking, criminal conduct or terrorist activity.*
- **Assistance** – *If any person helps another person to launder the proceeds of drug trafficking or criminal conduct, or to launder terrorist funds, he/she will be committing an offence. Any of the following will constitute an offence:*
   - *To obtain, use or undertake any act in relation to property which represents the proceeds of illegal activity.*
   - *To assist a person to retain control over, ownership of, or the benefits from the proceeds of illegal activity.*
   - *To hide or transfer property out of the UK or to assist a person to do so for the purpose of avoiding prosecution and/or the making of a confiscation order in relation to that property.*

   However, someone committing the above offences must do more than just commit the act of assistance. They must do so knowing or suspecting that the property or person they are assisting is connected to criminal activity. In the case of terrorism the person must have either known or had reasonable cause to suspect that the funds or the person they are assisting have been engaged in terrorist activities.

   In the case of terrorist funds a person can be found guilty of the offence of assisting if the prosecution is able to prove that the person either knew or ought reasonably to have known about the origins of those terrorist funds.

Happily, it is a defence to these offences if a person disclosed his knowledge or belief concerning the origins of the property, either to the police or the appropriate person with his employer.

The maximum penalties for any offence of assisting a money launderer are 14 years imprisonment and/or unlimited fine.

- **Failure to report** – *If an employee suspects money laundering he must inform the police or his employer as soon as possible. If he fails to do so as soon as is reasonably practicable he will be committing criminal offence. The relevant legislation specifically provides that any employee making a disclosure of this kind will not be in breach of any duty of confidentiality owed to a customer. The offence is punishable with a maximum of five years' imprisonment. Where an employee does report their concerns they must not be careful not to alert the suspicions of the alleged launderer as this itself is an offence – 'tipping off'.*

- **Tipping off** – *The offence of tipping off is committed if:*
  o *Prejudicial information (that which could harm the case) is disclosed to any third party, not just the person suspected of money laundering.*
  o *If prejudicial information is disclosed to a third party who is aware that a report of a suspicious transaction has been made either to the police or to the employer.*
  o *These offences are punishable with a maximum of five years' imprisonment and/or an unlimited fine.*

6.3   Reporting a suspected case of money laundering

Think

Consider these examples of possible money laundering:

A 17-year-old youth deposits large amounts of cash once a week and draws a smaller amount once a week. What is he up to?
Could be drugs dealing?

A businessman receives large payments from abroad and similar amounts go out to another foreign bank account on the same day? Where is the money going?
Could be part of a layering operation?

A young woman wants some investment advice. She has a large amount of cash to invest. Where did the money come from?
Could be the proceeds of crime?

In each of the above there may well be a plausible explanation, however, all three do seem suspicious.

If you suspect someone of money laundering there will be a procedure that you can follow that your organisation will have laid down for your protection. Remember that the penalties for becoming involved in money laundering are high and you, *not* your employer, could be liable. However, the following points should always be remembered:

- *If you are suspicious then do not say anything about your concerns to the customer – you could be accused of 'tipping them off'.*
- *Report the case immediately to the person in your organisation who is responsible for investigating money laundering allegations. You will usually be expected to provide details of the transactions that alerted you. This investigating officer will then take the matter out of your hands and be able to confirm or deny your claim.*

7.0
Fraud

Fraud has been occurring for as long as there have been financial services institutions and in many different guises. It was once described as a 'white collar' crime, however, it is now recognised as an unacceptable cost to society. Whether an individual has their credit card details 'skimmed' or a financial services provider has their computer system abused to hide a multi-million pound fraud, everyone suffers. Both the organisation and the customer feel the effects of institutional fraud. Customers suffer indirectly as they will be subject to price rises to cover the costs to the organisation of the fraud or by the inconvenience of more rigorous procedures in account opening. There will be significant repercussions following the events of 11 September 2001 air disasters in New York in an effort to reduce anti-terrorism.

The government estimates that the total cost of all fraud losses are costing the UK economy 17 times the value of burglaries. However, it is not a subject that lends itself to hard and fast data. The British Bankers Association have conducted a confidential survey to try to establish the extent of fraud with respondents responsible for over 50% of the banking business done in the UK.

The survey showed that the financial services industry is trying to grapple with conflicting objectives. Fiduciary duties mean that the recovery of funds takes priority. This can be at odds with public duties to aid the eventual prosecution of criminal activity. Shareholder interests and reputational pressures can increase the need for secrecy whilst it may be more in the public interest to disclose full details, whatever the effect of the share price. Balancing these needs requires careful judgment.

This section deals with the main types of fraud that personal customers may become exposed to and how you can help them avoid becoming the victim. As technology improves to combat crime through fraud, so does the ability of the criminals to overcome the barriers put in their way. Members of staff and customers can do much by being vigilant and careful with their cheque books, plastic cards and banking details and taking care when accounts are opened that all the procedures are properly carried out.

Think

Consider the following question:

> What types of fraud can you think of that customers can be exposed to?
>
>
>
> What types of fraud are financial services providers exposed to?

7.1 Cheque fraud – there are various ways that customers and the financial services providers can become exposed to fraud:

- *A cheque that has been genuinely signed by the customer but has been added to, or altered. It may be where the payee (the person who the cheque is made out to) has increased the amount of the cheque by inserting words or figures. It could be that the cheque has been stolen and the name of the payee changed to allow it to be paid into the thief's bank account.*
- *It could be that the chequebook has been stolen (either from an insecure address such as a rented property, or from the post, or it has been stolen from the customer) and the thief forges the customer's signature and uses the forgeries to pay for good and services. Customers can be subject to quite serious muggings when they*

have chequebooks stolen and even a simple theft where a pickpocket takes property without the customer knowing can still be quite distressing.

To prevent fraud of this types there are various actions that customers can take:

- *Any alterations to cheques must come from all parties liable on the cheque, i.e. the person whose account the cheque is drawn on. An unauthorised alteration constitutes a material alteration and renders the cheque void. This means that the bank would be unable to debit the customers account. Customers are expected to take usual and reasonable precautions to prevent forgeries when they write out cheques. This can be by writing words and figures to the far left-hand side of the appropriate place on cheques and any space remaining to the right filled with a line.*

- *Customers should be discouraged from leaving signed, blank, cheques for the payee to complete. If it is absolutely necessary to do this the customer should write across the top of the cheque, words such as 'not to exceed one hundred pounds' if this is the amount the cheque is to be limited to.*

The bank should not pay the cheque if there has been an obvious alteration that has not been signed for by the customer. The two tests that can be used in the instance of fraudulent alteration are:

- *Did the customer exercise reasonable care in drawing the cheque?*
- *Was the alteration detectable by the bank?*

If the answer to both questions is 'no' the customer must bear the loss. If the answer to either is 'yes' the loss falls on the bank.

Another way that fraud can happen is through stopped cheque (or countermand) orders. It is a bank's duty and authority not to pay a cheque that has been stopped by a customer. Obviously a customer must give notice to the bank that the cheque is to be stopped in good time and often customers will telephone their instructions. Orders to stop cheques must be very clear and in particular if the customer can confirm which number cheque the order relates to this is helpful. In practice, however, stop orders can give rise to a number of problems:

- *Details can be mis-heard over the phone and the wrong cheque can be stopped.*
- *Agreeing to stop a cheque that is backed by a cheque card. The customer agrees not to stop cheques that are backed by a cheque card and a bank may be within its rights not to stop the cheque even when it has taken stop instructions. Staff may wish to check with the customer that they had not used their cheque card with the cheque.*
- *The bank inadvertently pays a stopped cheque and as a result wrongfully dishonours another cheque.*

- *The bank receives notice from a payee that the cheque has been lost. The bank can only stop the cheque on the instructions of the drawer of the cheque (i.e. its customer).*
- *The bank receives notice of the stop, which is later cancelled. If the bank subsequently fails to pay the cheque it is liable for breach of contract.*

This shows that staff need to be very careful to take stop instructions collecting as much detail as possible and to ensure that the details are recorded on the customers account as soon as possible.

7.2   Plastic card fraud – Card fraud cost the UK £292.6 million in 2000 an increase of 55% on 1999's figure of £188.4 million. Some types of fraud are growing rapidly, especially counterfeit fraud and card-not-present fraud, which is committed using the telephone, mail order or the Internet. However, to put the fraud increases in context, the increase in the number of cards issued and their usage is still growing and fraud losses against turnover is .0145%. However, this still is a major headache for the financial institutions and a huge inconvenience for those people whose cards or card details are used fraudulently.

To combat crime two things need to be established a the time of the transaction:

- *Is the card genuine?*
- *Is the person using it the true owner?*

The following examples show the types of fraud and show ways that customers can look out for it happening to them:

- *Counterfeit fraud – a counterfeit card is one either that has been printed, embossed or encoded without permission from the issuer, or one which has been issued and then altered or re-coded. Most cases of this type of fraud involve 'skimming', a process where the genuine data in the magnetic stripe on one card is electronically copied onto another, without the cardholder's knowledge. Skimming tends to occur at retail outlets, quite often in restaurants and petrol stations. The attendant copies the customer's card details, before handing it back to the customer and then sells these details on higher up the criminal ladder. To combat this type of fraud it is vital that the cardholders check their statements for any transactions that are not theirs.*
- *Fraud on the phone, mail order or Internet transactions – These are known as 'card-not-present' frauds where neither the card nor its owner are present at the point of sale. This crime usually involves fraudulently obtained card details to make a purchase. These details can be obtained by the fraudster from discarded receipts. It is also possible for fraudsters to use computer software to randomly generate credit card account numbers for card-not-present transactions. A new address and card security code system is being introduced to combat this,*

however, customers must take care not to carelessly discard receipts and check their statements for any unfamiliar transactions.

- *Lost or stolen cards – most fraud on these cards occurs at retail outlets even before the customer is aware that the card has been stolen. To help combat this a 'hot card file' system is used to distribute data about lost or stolen cards to 80,000 UK retailers to alert them to missing cards. It is very important to make sure that cardholders report any losses as soon as possible so that their details can go onto this system and a block put on their card.*

- *Mail non-receipt – this is where customers cards go missing in the post and it was, at one point, attributable for 20% of card losses. The banking industry then teamed up with the Royal Mail to monitor and control card distribution which has accounted for a sharp decline in this type of fraud.*

- *ATM fraud – the majority of fraud of this type is where the cardholder has written down their PIN (personal identification number) and kept it with their card, in their purse or wallet and this is then stolen. Some cases also occur through 'shoulder surfing' where criminals look over the cardholder's shoulder when they are using the ATM and then steal the card. Customer should never write down their PIN and always be alert when using a cash machine.*

7.3   Shopping on the Internet – most Internet fraud involves using card details fraudulently obtained to make card-not-present transactions. Currently this type of fraud is low, accounting for approximately 2% of all card fraud losses. The incidence of hackers stealing cardholder data from websites is very low compared with the other types of fraud. However, to protect data the international cardholder schemes have stringent criteria for how retailer websites protect and store card information.

To protect against the possibility that a hacker will intercept cardholder data in transit through the Internet, certified organisations 'encrypt' (encode) the data as it travels. Some top tips for customers concerned about Internet shopping:

- *Keep a record of the retailer's contact details and be careful if there is nothing more that the website details.*

- *Click on the security icon of the retailer to check that they have an encryption certificate. Only use companies that have this certificate and use secure transaction technology.*

- *Check your statements as soon a you receive them. Raise queries on any transactions you are unsure about.*

- *Never disclose your PIN to anyone, even people purporting to be from the bank.*

- *If you are dubious about giving your card details find another method of payment.*

7.4 *Account opening fraud* – there are a number of ways that fraud can occur at account opening. These are to do with fraudsters supplying false names and addresses. They will then make applications for loans, sometimes multiple applications, which they subsequently default on. They may also pay in fraudulently altered cheques and draw cash before the cheques is returned unpaid.

It is very important that to prevent this type of fraud that account opening staff are satisfied with the identity of account holders and that internal systems are able to detect multiple applications.

Index

Financial services institutions/
  organisations
  authorised firms, 48
  codes of conduct, 50
  customer challenges, meeting, 116
  customers –
    needs, meeting, 28–34
    reaching, 32
  differentiation of, 32
  distribution channels, 103–108
  ethics, 34–36
  European Union, issues relating to, 19
  exempt organisations, 48
  external demands and customer
    preferences, meeting, 105
  liquid funds, 11
  London-based, 21
  marketing by, 32
  opportunities, taking advantage of 111, 112
  percentage of funds deposited, 12
  reserve asset ratio, 12
  resourcing issues, 116–119
  retail organisations, 22–24
  shareholders, provisions for, 11
  social responsibility, 34–36
  specialised goods and products, 21
  suppliers, 116–119
Financial Services Ombudsman Service
  complaints to, 144, 145
  ombudsmen in, 145
Financial services products
  investment, definition, 38
  non-regulated –
    cheque accounts, 88
    non-authorised staff, sale by, 88
    regulated distinguished, 38–41
    savings accounts, 88
    statutory provisions, 37
  packaged, 48
  range of, 94
  regulated –
    Individual Savings Accounts (ISAs),
    70. See also INDIVIDUAL
    SAVINGS ACCOUNTS (ISAS)

  life assurance as, 59. See also LIFE
    ASSURANCE
  mortgages, associated with, 76
  non-regulated distinguished, 38–41
  pensions as, 52. See also PENSIONS
  personal protection insurance as, 63.
    See also PERSONAL
    PROTECTION INSURANCE
  statutory provisions, 37
Fiscal policy
  meaning, 4
  objectives, 15
Fraud
  account opening, in relation to, 163
  cheque, 159–161
  cost of, 158
  existence of, 158
  Internet shopping, relating to, 162
  plastic card, 161, 162
  types of, 159

Gilt-edged stocks
  borrowing by, 26
Government policies
  Budget, 119, 120
  impact of, 119
  legislation, in, 120

House prices
  relevance of, 15
Human rights
  European Convention, 149

Income
  disposable, amount of, 16
  distribution, inflation affecting, 10
Individual Savings Accounts (ISAs)
  components of, 70
  Maxi, 70
  Mini, 70
  purpose of, 69
  regulated product, as, 70
  standards, 71